REALMS: ***The Environment That Determines What Responds*** by Dr. Marlene Miles

Freshwater Press 2026

ISBN: 978-1-971933-55-9

Paperback Version

Table of Contents

REALMS

YOU ARE NOT JUST IN A PLACE

There are things that should be working that are not. There are efforts that should be producing that are failing. There are people who are doing less than you and seeing more than you.

This is where frustration begins. When results do not match effort, the natural response is to increase effort. Work harder. Pray longer. Push more. But what if the issue is not effort? What if the issue is environment?

You are not just living in a place. You are functioning in an environment that is not always visible. It is not announced and does not introduce itself, but it is always speaking. It determines what grows easily, what struggles constantly, what is resisted, and what is allowed without effort.

Some people have called this, *atmosphere*. Others have called it, *spiritual climate*. But this is more precise than that. This is not just what you feel. This is what is in operation.

You can walk into a space where things move quickly, doors open easily, and connections form naturally. You can also walk into another space where everything is delayed, everything is resisted, and everything must be forced. The difference is not always the person. The difference is the environment.

This is why two people can do the same thing and get completely different results. You have seen two people in the same business; one is successful, the other is not. It is why there are rich doctors and also poor doctors. It may explain why there are rich businessmen and others who struggle.

Personally, this could be why something can work for a person in one season and stop working in another. It is why effort alone is not a reliable strategy, because effort does not override what is already in operation.

You can have the right idea, the right timing, and the right intention, and still struggle. Not because you are wrong, but because you are planted in an environment that does not support what you are trying to produce.

This book is not about effort. This book is about understanding where you are operating from. Once you understand environments, you will stop overexerting, misdiagnosing, and fighting the wrong battles.

You will begin to recognize that some things are not difficult, they are simply not supported where you are. And once you see that, you will stop trying to force results and start changing environments.

A REALM IS NOT A PLACE — IT IS A CONDITION

A realm is often mistaken for a place, as though it were something you could locate on a map or enter by movement. A realm is not defined by geography. It is defined by condition. It is the unseen environment that governs what is allowed, what is resisted, and what responds.

You can stand in the same room as another person and not be operating in the same realm. You can share space, share conversation, even share opportunity, and still experience completely different outcomes. This is because a realm is not determined by where you are standing, but by what is in operation around you.

A realm is a condition that has been established, whether intentionally or not. It is sustained by agreement, reinforced by repetition, and maintained by what is allowed to remain. It does not announce itself, yet it is always present. It speaks without words, and its language is results. This is why some environments seem to "work" for certain people and not for others. It is not always about intelligence, effort, or even timing. It is about condition. A realm either supports what you are doing, or it resists it.

Many have called this "atmosphere," but atmosphere is often treated as something emotional or temporary. A realm is more stable than that. It is not simply what you feel when you enter a space. It is what consistently functions there, whether you feel it or not. A place can change quickly. A realm does not. It must be established, and once established, it continues until something disrupts it or replaces it. This is why people can move locations and still experience the same patterns. They have changed places, but they have not changed realms.

A realm is not where you *are*, it is what is **governing where you are.**

For example, an oven is a realm where brownies or cookies will bake. The refrigerator is also a realm, but it does not bake brownies. It's an entire other realm. As a baker you could prepare everything correctly, measuring the ingredients, following the recipe exactly and still produce nothing. The cookies are prepared and on the baking sheet, but if you put them in the refrigerator or leave them on the counter, you will not produce cookies that are useable and edible. You placed or left them in the wrong realm.

The oven supports transformation. The refrigerator preserves what already is. Both are functioning properly, but they are not interchangeable. You don't fix a refrigerator to make it bake. You move what you're doing into the **right realm.**

Many people are trying to produce results in environments that are not designed for what they are attempting. For example, a person starts a business in the exact location where two businesses (same type business) have already failed. There are a lot of variables, but the idea of realm should be considered.

If a guy goes fishing in the exact spot, same time every day for a week and catches nothing --, there are still variables, but realm should be considered. Peter fished in the same spot all night and caught nothing. Jesus told them to drop their nets on the other side. That is not a change in realms as in the water, but JESUS changed things as we will see later in this book. Jesus operated in full authority because all power and authority was given to Him. Not only that, he exercised jurisdiction in the Earth. Jesus could even send a Word and heal.

So instead of just increasing effort, questioning your business model or assuming you did something wrong. Look at realm. If there may be nothing wrong with the process, then the realm must be considered. Is the realm wrong for the desired outcome?

Some environments are not built for what you are trying to produce. Period.

Realms determine what functions.

REALMS HAVE LAWS WITHOUT ANNOUNCEMENTS

Every realm operates by laws, but those laws are rarely spoken. They are not posted, explained, or negotiated. They are revealed through patterns.

If something consistently works, there is a law supporting it. If something consistently fails, there is a law opposing it. These laws do not require your awareness to function. They do not wait for your agreement. They simply operate.

This is where many become frustrated. They are trying to produce results without understanding the laws of the realm they are in. They apply effort, increase pressure, and even refine their methods, but nothing changes. Not because their effort is wrong, but because the law in operation does not support their outcome.

A realm of provision operates by different laws than a realm of lack. A realm of Peace operates by different laws than a realm of confusion. If you do not discern the law, you will misinterpret the resistance.

You may think you are being attacked when you are simply operating *outside* of what is supported. You may think something is wrong with you, when in reality, you are functioning in a realm whose laws do not favor what you are trying to produce.

Laws within a realm do not argue. They do not adjust themselves to your desire. They remain consistent. This consistency is what gives a realm its power. It creates predictability. Over time, that predictability becomes expectation.

People begin to say, “This is just how things go.” “This is how it always happens.” “This is normal.” But what they are calling normal is simply a law they have stopped questioning. A realm does not need to explain itself. It only needs to repeat itself.

Authority operates from a throne, but it expresses through a realm. A throne gives you the right to rule. A realm determines what actually responds. Realms are operational environments where laws, permissions, and responses are consistent. A realm tells you what works, what grows, what dies, what is resisted, and what is allowed without effort.

If it doesn’t work, hasn’t worked and keeps not working no matter what you do, maybe you don’t need more effort. Perhaps you need a different realm.

A realm is not your reach. A realm is not your jurisdiction. These terms are often used interchangeably, but they are not the same. Don’t confuse them, else the entire situation could be misdiagnosed. A realm is the **environment you are functioning in**. Your **reach** is how far your influence extends. Your **jurisdiction** is where you have the legal right to act.

A realm is what determines what actually *responds*. You can have reach without results. You can have jurisdiction without manifestation if you are operating in a realm that does not support what you are trying to do.

You can be authorized to act in a place and still be resisted by the realm you are in.

A person can have the authority to build, the wisdom to build, the resources to build, …and still nothing holds if they are functioning in a realm of resistance to that particular outcome. Jurisdiction gives you permission. A realm gives you cooperation—or opposition.

Jurisdiction is *legal standing, but the* Realm is the *operating conditions of the court*. You can walk into a court where you belong……and still encounter a hostile atmosphere. A throne may authorize you, but a realm decides how easily that authority moves. Your reach tells you how far you can go. Your jurisdiction tells you where you're allowed to function, but your realm determines what actually yields.

YOU ARE ALREADY FUNCTIONING IN ONE

No one is outside of a realm. No one is operating in neutral space. Whether recognized or not, every person is functioning within a realm that is producing consistent results. You do not have to choose a realm for it to exist. It is already in operation. The only question is whether you are aware of it.

This is why some people cannot explain their outcomes. They can describe what they are doing, but they cannot explain why it is or is not working. They are engaging actions without understanding the environment those actions are taking place in.

A person may say, "I am doing everything right." That may be true. Right actions in the wrong realm do not produce the intended result. When effort is present, but results are absent, the natural conclusion is that something must be wrong with the effort. So, the person adjusts, increases, or intensifies what they are doing. The issue is not always what is being done, sometimes the issue is where it is being done.

You are already functioning in a realm that is producing patterns in your life. Thee patterns are seen in what comes easily and what requires force. Most often this is first seen your father's house. as a child or young person still living at home you may have looked at your parents and said, When I grow up my life won't be like that. Or you have wondered why they are *like that*.

It's the realm, the familial realm.

Simply wanting to change it or wishing it with be different, even if you made yourself a promise that you'd change the patterns and outcomes of your own adult life doesn't mean you will. Well, you can if you recognize what a realm is and how it works.

If you don't do any realm work, those patterns will most likely repeat and you will get the same or similar results that your parents (for example) got, no matter how much you hated those results growing up. Well, except for the Mercy of God.

If you do not identify the realm, you will continue to misinterpret the pattern. If you misinterpret the pattern, you will continue to apply solutions that do not work. Then you will continue getting the same results that those who came before you got.

Realms are not entered through desire. Neither are they changed or transformed just because you want them to. They are not accessed through emotion. Wanting something does not place you in a realm where that thing functions.

This is where many make a critical error. They feel strongly about a change, and they interpret that *feeling* as movement. They believe that because they desire a different outcome, they have already shifted into having the thing they desire. If they know nothing of realms they cannot shift into a different one, except, again, by the Mercy of God.

Desire does not establish environment.

Emotion can motivate action, but it does not override conditions. You can feel ready and still be unsupported. You can feel confident and still be resisted. You can feel certain and still be out of alignment with the realm you are in.

This is why emotional momentum often collapses. It is not sustained by structure. It is not reinforced by law. It is driven by feeling, and feeling does not establish a realm.

Realms are entered through alignment, not emotion. They are established through what is consistently allowed, reinforced, and maintained. Not what is briefly felt. This is also why temporary change does not last. A person can adjust behavior for a moment, but if the realm remains unchanged, the environment will eventually pull them back into what is normal for that realm.

Realms do not respond to moments; they respond to what is sustained.

A realm does not ask how you feel. It responds to what is in operation. Until that is understood, a person will continue trying to change results, without ever changing the realm those results are coming from.

AGREEMENT BUILDS WHAT YOU LIVE IN

Realms are not accidental. They are formed through agreement.

Agreement is not limited to what is spoken out loud. It is not confined to formal decisions or declared positions. Agreement is established through what is accepted, what is repeated, and what is allowed to continue without interruption.

You can disagree with something in words… and still be in agreement with it in practice. Whatever you consistently agree with—whether consciously or not—begins to shape the environment you function in.

Agreement is not only spiritual — it is also practical. When people hear the word agreement, they often think only in spiritual terms. Agreement with God. Agreement with truth. Agreement with what is right.

That is one level, but agreement also happens between people, within systems, inside patterns of behavior, and through repeated participation.

A realm can be formed through spiritual alignment, and it can also be formed through relational and behavioral consistency.

AGREEMENT WITH THE SPIRIT

There are realms that are established through alignment with the Spirit of God. These realms are marked by clarity, order, provision, Peace, and consistency that does not require strain. They are not formed by effort alone. They are formed by alignment with God.

When a person consistently agrees with Truth, walks in obedience, and maintains that alignment, an environment begins to form around them where certain things function naturally. Doors open without force. Understanding comes without confusion. Provision meets need without constant struggle. We may call this Grace or Divine favor. This is not coincidence. This is a realm responding to alignment.

AGREEMENT WITH WHAT IS NOT OF GOD

Agreement does not have to be righteous to be effective. A person can come into agreement with negative things too, such as fear, lack, confusion, compromise, or disorder. How so? By their wrong thoughts or by evil confession they say, invite and tell these things to have a seat and stay a while. Many times, it is done in jest or in self-deprecation.

Stop it, please. Only say about yourself what God says about you. Else, over time, those agreements establish a realm just as consistently. If fear is consistently agreed with, a realm of fear is established. If lack is constantly reinforced, a realm of lack forms. If confusion is tolerated, a realm of confusion stabilizes. These realms do not require intention; they only require agreement.

AGREEMENT WITH PEOPLE

Realms are also formed through agreement with other individuals. This is where many overlook what they are participating in. When people consistently interact, align, and reinforce the same patterns, they begin to create a shared environment. That environment becomes predictable. It develops its own norms, its own expectations, and its own limitations.

In some circles, progress is normal, growth is supported, movement is expected. However, in others, stagnation is normal, limitation is reinforced, and advancement is resisted

The difference is not always individual capability; it is collective agreement. This is especially noticeable when people grow up in certain cultures (realms) where good things often or always happen or bad things take the fore. Expectation and faith are weighing in here.

ASSOCIATION MATTERS. You are not only influenced by what you believe. You are influenced by what you consistently agree with in others. If you remain in agreement with dysfunction, limitation, or disorder, you will find yourself functioning within a realm that reflects those agreements. If you allow it and never interrupt it, it remains. **You can agree by agreeing. You can also agree by not disagreeing.**

REPETITION ESTABLISHES WHAT AGREEMENT STARTED

Agreement begins the process, and repetition stabilizes it. What is done once does not form an environment; what is done repeatedly does. This is how environments become predictable, not because of a single moment, but because of sustained pattern.

Over time, repetition removes resistance. What was once uncomfortable becomes normal. What was once questioned becomes accepted, and once it is accepted, it becomes part of the environment.

Agreement and repetition can form a pattern, but authority is what gives that pattern permission to remain. Authority does not always look like leadership. It can be subtle, expressed in what is permitted, reinforced, or left unchallenged. When something is allowed to continue without interruption, it gains stability, and what gains stability begins to define the environment.

Every environment is built through what is allowed, not just what is chosen intentionally, but what is permitted consistently. This is why two people can be in similar situations and experience completely different outcomes. One interrupts what should not remain, while the other tolerates it. One establishes boundaries, while the other allows overflow.

Over time, those decisions do not just affect behavior. They build environments. Environments are not built in a day; they are built in what you tolerate.

In the Garden, everything functioned. There was no resistance. There were no thorns, no breakdowns, no instability. What was established held. What was intended produced. The environment responded because alignment was intact.

After the Fall, resistance entered. The ground no longer responded the same way. What once worked easily now required toil. What once held began to break down. Not because the design was wrong, but because alignment was lost.

From that point forward, everything reflected that misalignment. Effort increased, but response decreased. Structure weakened. Environments became unstable. What should have held no longer did.

This is why Jesus did not enter environments and struggle with them. He entered, and things aligned. Storms ceased. Disorder corrected. What was out of place responded. He did not adjust to the environment; the environment responded to Him.

Creation recognized alignment and bowed. This didn't happen because Jesus forced it, but because there was nothing in Him that contradicted what He carried. He was fully aligned, fully established, and fully authorized. There was no internal misalignment that could weaken what He brought into a space.

What He carried was so established that disorder had no place to remain. This is what structure looks like when it is correct. Everything that is built depends on Structure.

You can increase effort, but effort does not fix misalignment. You can reinforce what is visible, but if the foundation is off, what you reinforce will still fail. You can continue to build, but if what you are building on is not set correctly, it will not hold.

The issue is not always what you are doing. The issue is whether what you are building on is aligned. The Carpenter's Son shows us that structure is not optional. It is essential. What is aligned holds. What is misaligned fails.

A REALM DOES NOT REQUIRE YOUR AWARENESS TO FORM

You do not have to understand this process for it to be working. Realms form whether you are intentional or not. This is why people can look up one day and realize they are in an environment they never meant to build. Nothing dramatic happened. No single moment defined it. It was built slowly, through agreement, through repetition, through allowance.

Once established, it begins to function as if it has always been there.

We all should be amazed at how God created man. We are complex. Many try to simplify what should remain appreciated or studied in its complexity. Sometimes complexity is warfare; sometimes it's confusion, but not everything that is complex is confusion. Confusion disorients. Complexity requires discernment. Confusion removes clarity. Complexity demands maturity. Too many have been taught to treat both as the same.

Anything that requires thought is dismissed. Anything that requires patience is avoided. Anything that cannot be immediately explained is labeled unnecessary.

In an effort to make things easier, what is actually necessary has been reduced. Not everything was designed to be simple. God did not create man as a shallow being.

He created man with depth, with layers and with capacity. Man has the ability to discern, to process, to recognize patterns, and to respond to what is not immediately visible. This is the man that God is mindful of. Man was not created to function on one level. There is what is seen, what is perceived, what is understood, and what is discerned although they are not the same, when these are collapsed into one, discernment is lost.

Trying to reduce everything to what is immediately visible or easily explained will not serve us well.

Realms are not always visible. You observe what consistently happens. You recognize patterns. You notice what works and what does not. You discern what is supported and what is resisted. This requires more than reaction. It requires attention.

SOMETIMES COMPLEXITY IS WARFARE

There are situations where things become unnecessarily complicated. What should be straightforward becomes layered. What should be clear becomes tangled. What should move easily becomes delayed.

This is not always natural.

Sometimes, complexity is introduced as resistance. To slow movement. To create fatigue. To produce frustration. When this happens, people often respond by withdrawing.

They disengage. They abandon what they were building. They step back, not because they were wrong… but because it became too difficult to navigate. This is one-way realms of resistance maintain themselves; not always through direct opposition, but through complication.

SOMETIMES COMPLEXITY IS DESIGN

Not all complexity is opposition. Some things are complex because they are meant to be handled with care.

Some things require attention, patience, and development. Not everything is meant to be accessed quickly. Not everything is meant to be handled casually.

There are realms that respond only to those who are willing to engage beyond the surface. This is where discernment becomes necessary. Because if you treat design like warfare, you will resist what you should learn.

If you treat warfare like design, you will tolerate what you should confront.

REALMS CAN BE RECOGNIZED BY WHAT THEY CONSISTENTLY PRODUCE

You may not always be able to define a realm immediately. But you can observe its patterns. A realm reveals itself through consistency. **A realm of provision:** Things come together. Needs are met without constant strain. There is movement without force.

A realm of lack: Effort is constant. Results are minimal. What is gained does not remain.

A realm of Peace: Decisions are clear. Movement is steady. There is no internal pressure to force outcomes.

A realm of confusion: Nothing settles. Everything feels uncertain. Even simple decisions become difficult.

A realm of access: Connections form easily. Doors open without excessive effort. There is movement across spaces that would normally be restricted.

A realm of resistance: Everything requires force. Progress is slow. What should be simple becomes difficult. These are not labels. These are patterns.

You do not have to name a realm to be affected by it. Many are waiting to fully understand something before they respond to it. But recognition does not always require definition. You may not be able to explain a realm in technical terms, yet you can see what it is producing. What it is producing tells you what you are in.

This is where many misdiagnose their situation. They assume they are the problem, that their effort is insufficient, or that their timing is off. When in reality, they are functioning in an environment that does not support what they are trying to produce. Who would try to naturally grow tropical fruits in the winter in Alaska? So, they adjust themselves instead of questioning the environment. We could say this is logical to look at temperature and environment, and it is, but realms are not visible. The results are visible, but not the realm itself.

Not everything difficult is warfare. Not everything complex is confusion. But everything consistent is a clue. God did not create you to function blindly. You were not designed to move through life guessing. You were designed to recognize, to discern, and to observe what is happening beyond what is immediately visible. This is not overcomplication; this is capacity. If capacity is ignored, everything begins to feel confusing. Not because it is unclear, but because it is being oversimplified.

The goal is not to make everything simple. The goal is to make things clear. Clarity does not remove depth; it reveals it. And once you can see clearly, you will stop reacting to what is happening and start recognizing the environment you are in.

ARE THERE REALMS THAT ARE NOT OF GOD?

Not every realm is aligned with God. Some environments are established through disorder, deception, fear, lack, or sustained compromise. These are functional but not neutral. A realm does not have to be righteous to be effective. It only has to be established and it will start producing. If it produces consistently, it is functioning—whether it is aligned with God or not.

A Believer does not lose identity by entering the wrong environment… …but they can experience the effects of it. You can be called, anointed, and aware, but still function in a realm that resists what God has placed in you.

Your identity does not change—but your environment can still affect your results. PEOPLE assume that If I belong to God, everything around me should automatically respond. But that is not always the case. Alignment determines response. For example, if being saved and Spirit-filled you decide to go into a hellish place, not being sent, but to party, you have stepped into a realm that is governed by something other than godliness. The Holy Spirit may tell you to get out of there, well at least once, but if you are trying to run away from the Voice of God, then He just may not speak to you again in that place. This is true if you are quenching or grieving Him. This is a different realm. God still knows where you are and He still has authority over that place, but if the people in nightclubs and bars could hear or even listen to the Holy Spirit, there would be no nightclubs or bars.

There are realms that suppress clarity, delay progress, normalize confusion, reinforce lack, or resist growth. Not because God designed them that way……but because they have been established through sustained agreement with what is not of Him.

Should believers remain there? No—not if they recognize it. You may enter an environment—but you are not called to remain in what contradicts what God is establishing in you.

This is not fear, avoidance, or superstition. This is discernment. Sometimes you are *sent* into an environment to disrupt it. Sometimes you are remaining in one that is disrupting you

Assignment is not the same as residence."

You can be *sent* into a place temporarily, but you are not meant to be shaped by what you were sent to confront. If you are consistently drained, resisted, or diminished, then you are not governing that environment; it is governing you.

A Believer is not called to fear environments. We are called to recognize them, discern them, and respond appropriately because not every place you can stand is a place you are meant to function from.

You are not called to adapt to every realm. Some you are called to leave. Some you are called to change.

REALMS THAT ARE NOT OF GOD

There are environments believers should not remain in. Evil realms have conditions of operation that are not aligned with God's order. Not every realm is aligned with God. Some environments are established through disorder, deception, fear, lack, or sustained compromise. These are not neutral; they are functional. They produce consistent outcomes.

A Believer can be *called*, anointed, aware and still function in a realm that resists what God has placed in you. Your identity does not change—but your environment can still affect your results.

ASTRAL TRAVEL VS. REALITY

The purpose of this chapter is to address the thought that people can jump from realm to realm.

Some say astral travel is not real, others say it is. The reason it is mentioned here is because our topic is realms. People who astral travel or say they do go to other realms. Since astral travel is not the sole subject of this book, I will give my own opinion and leave it there. You believe as you will.

I believe astral travel is possible and I believe it is demon-assisted. How did the devil take Jesus up to an exceedingly high mountain (Matthew 4)? Piggy back? Escalade? Airplane? Helicopter? No. Jesus allowed this because of His assignment. They went in the spirit.

I do not believe Jesus imagined His Wilderness Temptation.

Now, back to us humans. I believe astral projection is possible, it is demon assisted, yes, I'm repeating myself. I believe that people believe they are going places in the astral because they have given co-control of their bodies over to entities that they should not even be dealing with. Think of a demonic middleman. The person wants to go somewhere, see something and often DO something to someone, on the sly, secretly, at night and have no culpability. They want to be able to say, "No, I was at home in my own house, in my own bed. It wasn't me."

The human is licensing the demon to go do whatever (as them or in some masquerade) and then come back and basically give a report of what happened, but since this person has given over his own physical body to this demon, this demon can also make a person feel the feelings of that experience, so now the human thinks they went someplace else and did a thing.

The experience seems so real. All the while the astral projector has either slowly, inch by inch giving themselves over to the demonic, or they are on their way to fully being possessed and by permission. Meanwhile, if another human is involved, they will sense oppression or attack by a demon sent by a foolish human.

I am not saying that all this is okay if no other human is involved. It is a practice in mysticism and Christians aren't supposed to do that. Occultists do this, Shaman's, Eastern religions and others across the world in other 'religions' recommend, teach and use this practice.

Self-driven 'spiritual travel' is not for me. Now, if it's God, that's a whole different thing.

Ezekiel 8:3 *"...the Spirit lifted me up between the earth and the heaven, and brought me... to Jerusalem..."* Ezekiel is shown something. It's a vision-type experience. It reveals hidden conditions.

Daniel sees himself in another location –Shushan, (Daniel 8:1-2), again in the context of a vision. This is not casual movement, nor is it something he initiated.

In Revelation 21:10, we read: *"...he carried me away in the spirit to a great and high mountain..."* John is shown the New Jerusalem. Clearly "in the spirit" this is for revelation, not curious exploration. There is a whole lot of stuff out in the spirit realm that we should not go near, touch, listen to or have any dealings with.

Philip is "caught away" in Acts 8:39 after baptizing the Ethiopian. This one is more physical, this is immediate relocation for purpose.

All these were initiated by God with a specific purpose. not repeated as a lifestyle. not taught as something to pursue. When God shows something, it is for revelation—not experience. You do *not* see in Scripture people regularly traveling around. We do not see people learning to "visit realms." We do not see people initiating these experiences themselves. casual exploration of environments.

When Angels are involved they deliver messages, they execute instructions, they assist with God's purpose

They are not tour guides, realm navigators, or experience facilitators. Angels serve purpose—not curiosity. Heaven is not an amusement park. There are a handful of moments where someone is shown something positioned to see something, or moved for a purpose. But it is rare, directed, and not repeatable on demand. In Scripture, being shown something is an assignment—not an activity.

STUCK IN REALMS

When a minister says, "People get stuck in realms they can't get out of," are they talking about a literal place a person is trapped in like a room? Or are they only talking about patterns and environments that a person does not know how to break free from?

Is that what they mean?

Stuck in a realm might mean stuck in confusion, stuck in fear, stuck in cycles, such as delay, or other destructive patterns. People can be functionally stuck, meaning everything they try keeps producing the same result.

Really?

This kind of stuckness is real. They are in a sustained environment that they have not interrupted or exited.

Can they interrupt it? Can they leave it? On their own, or do they need help?

Jesus came to set the captives free.

What captives? All captives--, any whosoever will. There was no one in the New Testament who asked for healing from Jesus who didn't get it, by all accounts.

The wages of sin is death. Jesus came to take the keys of Death and the Grave. He led captivity captive. Jesus set those free who were even in Hades with no way to get out. Yes, He healed and delivered in His Earth ministry, but when He descended, that is when He set captives free.

His anointing was so great for this that even after Jesus was arrested, His anointing set Barrabas free. The people were chanting, “Give us Barrabas,” and I kinda betcha they didn’t know why.

It was the anointing. It was the Grace. It was the prophecy. It was the realm that Jesus carried. At the scene of Trial of Jesus who is innocent and Barabbas who is guilty. The crowd chooses: “Give us Barabbas.”

Barabbas didn’t just “get lucky,” he became a living demonstration of what Jesus came to do. This is substitution in motion. Before the cross even happens, the pattern is already visible. One man walks out of captivity… because another is about to take his place.

The crowd thought they were making a political choice, but heaven was executing a divine exchange. Jesus came to set the captives free, not by war or force, but by divine exchange.

Jesus came to set the captives free, so why are we confused when the captive walked?

Barabbas is not the anomaly. Barabbas is the example, his walking is the function of the assignment. Shadows healing (Acts 5:15, Peter) evidence of the overflow of the realm. Not as random miracles, but as environmental outcomes. When a realm is established, it produces outcomes without needing individual explanations for each one.

Barabbas walks because freedom entered the system. Shadows heal because power saturated the environment. Same source. Different expressions. Both Barabbas and Peter's shadow healing are evidence of capacity introduced into a realm. Barabbas walks. The sick are healed; even shadows carry effect.

So, Jesus came to set the captives free. Who was more captive than a soul in hell with no redemption and no way out?

> Shall the prey be taken from the mighty, or the lawful captive delivered?
>
> But thus saith the Lord, Even the captives of the mighty shall be taken away, and the prey of the terrible shall be delivered, (Isaiah 49:24-25A)

The wages of sin is death. It can, but death doesn't mean instantaneous, most of the time. God is Merciful, after all. Adam and Eve sinned and they died spiritually, but physically they were still walking about the Earth doing their thing, having kids and what not. They looked like they were still alive.

We know that what we see in the physical comes from the spiritual FIRST. The wages of sin is death. Who writes this on a Death Certificate, but the cause of death is usually, SIN.

On the way to hell to set the captives free, Jesus stopped along the way to heal people. That is, He stopped the process of death that had already started in the people who were sick who came to Him because sickness is the beginning of the process.

There were captives, lawfully in hell. You don't get stuck in a place unless you are in agreement with that place. Two cannot walk together unless they be agreed. Pre-Jesus at Golgotha those who had died and were in hell were in agreement with sin. That is what happened to them. They were stuck in the Realm of Hell because before Jesus, there was no way out. Don't get me wrong, even after Jesus and after physical death of the body, there is no way out. So, people need to make their decision for Christ on this side while they are still physically alive.

While still alive, you don't get trapped in realms. You remain in them through unbroken agreement. No realm holds you against your will, but many realms are sustained without your awareness. A person could get trapped in a mindset or be held by a stronghold and may be weakened to fight it on their own and therefore need help from a stronger or free Christian (minister).

We all need Jesus.

Jesus came to set the captives free yet there is no language in the Bible of Him 'going to realms to release people or be going off to some realms to get the people out?

Oh, but wait a minute, that's what He did, He went to the realm of Hell to set the captives free.

Why have we only thought the captives were the living people that Jesus encountered in His three years of ministry? Jesus healed every one of them. Every one of them. While Jesus was on the way to see about healing the 12-year-old girl, He got stopped along the way by the woman with the issue of blood. After the encounter with the woman who touched His hem, the servant told Him, (pretty much), "Never mind, she's dead now." Jesus continued on to the adolescent girl's house anyway and she was resurrected.

Jesus came to set the captives free. Everyone He came to set free was either dead or on their way to being dead. Without Jesus and the New Covenant, we all were. Don't let the irony escape you. God doesn't deal in dead things and Jews were forbidden to touch the dead. Jesus was Jewish. Anyone who was dead, was dead in sin and because of sin which means they were captives of sin. The wages of sin is death. Quickly or slowly, it is death, and it is the Law.

Jesus came to set the captives FREE, and on his way to hell to set them free, He was stopped by multitude after multitude. He was stopped by the sick, the blind, the lame, the halt, those who were bleeding out, dying, the mute, the deaf and those with many other infirmities.

Still, Jesus was on His way to do His assignment. He got stopped by Pharisees, Sadducees—all kinds of folks, but **He came to set the captives free, even the lawful captives.**

Who could be more captive than the soul of a man already in hell?

Yes, soul captivity is a real thing for the living. If the soul is captured it is tied, compromised, locked down and the devil is already counting. The wages of sin is death. The devil is counting and waiting. Yes, there are regions of captivity of the soul of a man, and he may not even know he is captive until he pays attention to the things in his life that have changed. Perhaps things in his life start dying before he sees that he is. His career, his health, his marriage… the wages of sin is death; after unrepented sin, something will die or start the process of dying.

A captive man could be in deep bondage at the level of the mind, will, and emotions (that is the soul). What the Bible calls strongholds, oppression, or captivity of thought and identity because death or the devil has begun the process of dragging that man. He doesn't want to be dragged. He wants to be saved. He wants to live. Even if he is deeply bound in patterns that feel like captivity, he still wants to live.

Books like *Regions of Captivity* (by Ana Farrell (which I love)) often use spatial language to describe layers of bondage, categories of oppression, or areas of life under control of certain patterns. So, when they say "region," they usually mean a consistent domain of influence. However, that author shows clear examples of people hiding out in caves and other real places and those people do need deliverance.

Wasn't Legion in a graveyard? Things that start in the spirit realm may cause or drive a man to act it out in the natural, eventually. A person is functioning within a *realm* that has established control over how they think, respond, and live and it may drive them to the limits, or they may be appearing to function normally in their own life while spiritually dysfunctional.

Captivity is not always relocation of the physical person, but it is sustained control. A person could be in real bondage, in a jail, prison or other locked area. When someone says, “If you go get them and don’t do it right, you can get stuck too,” what they may be *trying* to describe is entering someone else’s environment without discernment and authorization. You can’t just go bust a person out of jail.

How do we know that they aren't really in soul captivity in the spirit and therefore they exhibit the patterns that we see in the natural? We don’t have to choose between *they’re in captivity”* or *“they’re showing patterns.”* In Scripture, those are the same reality described two ways. Captivity shows up as patterns. Patterns are how captivity becomes visible. A realm is what’s in operation. Captivity is how a person is being held within it. Patterns are the evidence you can observe.

What is happening internally will eventually show externally. What is sustained within a person will repeat around them. You do not see captivity directly. You see what it produces. What it produces will repeat until something interrupts it. Captivity is the condition. Patterns are the evidence. You don’t need to claim the soul has traveled somewhere or is located in another place, to acknowledge real bondage.

Books and messages have been produced that interpret a man’s dreams for him and many indicate soul captivity. It’s why we need Biblical, Christian, accurate dream interpretation and to pray and act accordingly after understanding what our dreams are telling us.

Scripture already gives us the language:

- "taken captive" (2 Timothy 2:26)
- "strongholds" (2 Corinthians 10:4–5),
- "oppressed" (Luke 4:18)

These describe control, influence, and limitation of freedom. The only reliable way to diagnose it is consistent fruit over time.

If a person repeatedly returns to the same destructive outcome, cannot sustain clarity or progress, experiences the same resistance regardless of effort. then something is holding that pattern in place. Call it captivity, stronghold, or a resistant realm. The diagnosis comes from what is consistently produced. Captivity is recognized by patterns.

It is not, *"Are they in captivity, or is it just behavior?"* It is, *"What is producing this pattern—and why is it still holding?"* Whether you call it captivity or pattern, the question remains the same: What is sustaining this—and will it be allowed to continue? It is the realm that man is in, whether it is a Godly realm or not will be seen in the fruit of that man's life.

Jesus came to set the captives free; we should avail ourselves to His full ministry. Amen.

THE JESUS REALM

What do people mean when they say, “I just go talk to Jesus.” Or, “I can talk to angels whenever I want,” they are usually describing one of three different things—and these are not the same.

1. PRAYER / COMMUNION

A person is praying, speaking to God, expressing thoughts internally, sensing guidance or peace. Translation: “I speak to God, and I perceive His response.”

That is normal, Biblical, and available to every Believer. Men ought to always pray, but this is not physically visiting, having on-demand conversations like a phone call, or entering another realm to speak face-to-face at will.

2. INTERNAL DIALOGUE / IMAGINED INTERACTION

Some people visualize, imagine conversations, “hear” responses in their thoughts. It can feel very real. Engaging in an internal conversation that feels external. This is where things can become subjective, hard to verify, and easily misinterpreted. The experience is internal, not environmental. It is not really happening on the outside, but within them, it is happening. It is how they hear the Holy Spirit, and Amen.

3. LANGUAGE THAT SOUNDS STRONGER THAN THE REALITY.

Sometimes people say, "I go talk to Jesus." Do they mean they pray and feel close to Him? Maybe they are using language that sounds more direct than what is actually happening. But to the person hearing that they may really think this person actually talks with Jesus on the regular and that may be what the person wants another to believe.

Yes, we have access to God, we can pray anytime. We can commune with Him. Scripture does NOT teach that Believers casually "enter another realm and hold conversations on demand like travel. There is a difference between: communion with God and claims of controlled access to spiritual encounters. Communion is relational, consistent, and grounded in Truth. Controlled access suggests on-demand experience, personal control, or repeated entry into encounters.

God is Omnipresent, so why do you have to go anywhere to speak with Him? Further our bodies are supposed to be the temple of the Holy Spirit, so if you've seen Jesus (He said), then you've seen the Father and the Holy Spirit always points back to Jesus. So, if the Holy Spirit is resident in you, why do you have to go anywhere?

Access to God is given. Control over encounters is not. Else, wouldn't the Bible be account after account of pre or post incarnate Christ showing up everywhere?

Scripture shows that angels are real. they serve God and they are sent by Him. it does NOT teach that believers initiate conversations with any of God's Angels at will. Angels respond to God's instruction—not human summoning.

The enemy, we know is an impersonator and can turn himself into an angel of light. Therefore, we must discern every *spirit*.

People say they go talk to Jesus because they feel something real such as Peace, clarity, or the Presence of God. they interpret it as a direct encounter. They may use language that elevates the experience. God is accessible. Prayer is real. Communion is real.

We should not affirm words like, "I enter realms to talk to Jesus," or, "I summon angels to speak with me" You do not need to enter a realm to speak to God. He is already present. Relationship with God does not require access points. It requires alignment.

Not every experience of closeness is an encounter. Some are simply awareness. Not every suspected encounter with Jesus or Angels is real. There are familiar and impersonating *spirits* just waiting to deceive those who don't know.

Then there are the types of people who say, "I went to Jesus' house…" "I sat with Him…" "We walked and talked face to face…" These people talk about detailed, scene-based encounters.

There are three possible sources for that kind of experience:

1. VIVID INTERNAL IMAGERY (most common)

Some people have extremely strong visualization ability, immersive imagination, the ability to "see" scenes internally as if they are real. This can feel like being somewhere talking to someone, or interacting in a space. They are experiencing a highly vivid internal scene. If they are Believers, that scene may be centered on Jesus, shaped by what they believe, and very. emotionally meaningful.

This is still internal, not environmental.

2. DREAM / VISION-TYPE EXPERIENCES (less common, but real)

There *are* moments in Scripture where people had visions, people saw symbolic scenes, people encountered God in a way that was not physical. Notice those were initiated by God, not controlled by the person, not repeatable on demand.

A vision is given; it is not scheduled.

3. LANGUAGE THAT HAS DRIFTED INTO LITERAL CLAIMS

Sometimes people have an experience, then retell it in a more literal way over time. So, what began as "I felt like I was with Him becomes, "I went to His house." The language becomes more concrete than the experience actually was.

Jesus is real, relationship with Him is real, communion is real. However, there are some people who are fully deceived by a false Christ, *familiar spirits*, or by that angel of Light.

Then there are those that none of this happened at all, but they want to gain the confidence of Believers and they make this up.

I wasn't there, I don't know what anyone saw, so I ask the Holy Spirit to lead me into all Truth. And, Amen.

Scripture does not teach that Believers regularly go visit Jesus' physical "location" at will. It does not present that as a normal, repeatable practice. There are experiences that feel like encounters. There are moments that feel immersive, detailed, and real. Not every vivid experience is an actual relocation.

Detail does not prove location. A person may describe a place, a conversation, or a setting. Description does not mean they were physically present there. **An experience can be vivid without being external.**

INTERNAL vs EXTERNAL

Internal means experienced within the person.

External means functioning independently of them.

If the experience begins when they engage it, continues while they focus, and ends when they stop it is dependent on them; a realm is not. If the experience depends on you to begin, it is not a place you entered.

If people believe they can go "visit" Jesus at will, and return with conversations, their internal experience becomes unquestionable authority. When experience becomes authority, discernment is lost.

Not every experience is an *encounter*. Not every vivid moment is external. Not every detailed story reflects a real location.

You do not travel to meet Jesus. He is not distant. You do not need a location to have relationship. Vivid does not mean external. Detailed does not mean true. Those people are most likely experiencing internal imagery, interpreting it as external reality, and describing it literally.

VIVID IS NOT VERIFICATION

Not everything that feels real is real in the way it is being understood. There are experiences that are detailed, immersive, and emotionally convincing. They can include settings, conversations, movement, and interaction. **Vivid is not verification.**

The mind is powerful. It is capable of producing experiences that feel external. A person can see clearly, hear distinctly, and interact within a scene and their physical body doesn't leave where they are, but can we say where their spirit or soul went? *Spirits*, devils, demons enter and leave bodies so there is spiritual movement in this realm and perhaps across realms. That doesn't mean it is of God, but it can happen.

This does not make the experience meaningless, but it does mean it must be interpreted correctly. Clarity of experience does not determine the source of it.

WHEN DETAIL BECOMES AUTHORITY

The more detailed an experience is, the more convincing it becomes. People begin to trust what they saw, what they heard, and what they felt. Without questioning what produced it, or what sustains it. Over time, the experience itself becomes the authority.

When detail replaces discernment, error can enter.

A person may say "I went somewhere," "I spoke face to face," or, "I entered a place." That entire experience may have occurred within them, not around them An internal experience described as external one will always be misunderstood.

If every vivid experience is accepted as reality, imagination becomes location, perception becomes truth, and experience becomes proof. Once that happens there is no standard left to measure anything by. If experience cannot be questioned, it cannot be trusted.

What is real does not need to be dramatized to be true.

Not only that, so many times in the Bible when people encountered Jesus, He told them to *go, and tell no one.*

Well---,

THIS IS NOT STAR TREK

So far, we've pretty much established that average folks are not jumping realms like quantum leapers or others on sci-fi shows. There are those who describe their experiences in ways that sound cinematic. They speak of entering spaces, traveling through environments, and interacting within detailed settings. The descriptions are vivid, structured, and almost scene by scene, but what is being described often resembles cinema more than reality.

In shows and films like *Star Trek* and *Star Wars*, characters open portals, travel between dimensions, step into different worlds, and interact in constructed environments. These scenes are immersive, detailed, and believable, but they are not real. They are designed with sets, scripts, special effects, and controlled outcomes. Cinema creates environments you can see, but seeing something does not make it real.

When people describe experiences as though they traveled somewhere, entered a place, or sat within a setting, the language begins to mirror what has already been seen in film. Not because they are intentionally copying it, but because that is the closest reference point available to them. If it sounds like a scene, it may be a construction.

A realm is not a stage. It is not a set, a location you walk into, or a place revealed like a scene. It is not something you observe, explore, or describe visually. It is something you function within, recognize by outcome, and experience through response. A realm is not something you watch; it is something that responds.

This distinction matters because cinema is designed to show you something, immerse you in it, and make it feel real. Reality is not proven by how something looks; it is proven by what it produces, what it sustains, and what it continues. What looks real is not always real. What functions consistently is.

You do not need a scene, a setting, or a visual experience to understand what is happening around you. What is real will show itself in what continues. If something requires a scene to explain it, it may be cinema. If it produces consistent results, it is an environment.

There are also those who experience intense dreams. They see clearly, move through scenes, engage in conflict, and wake up feeling as though they have been somewhere. The experiences are vivid, lucid, frequent, and sometimes exhausting. Over time, a conclusion is formed that they are being taken somewhere, fighting in another realm, or even getting stuck there. This is especially true of repetitive dreams.

DREAMS ARE EXPERIENCES

A dream can feel real. It can include movement, interaction, confrontation, and emotion. Some say that the soul or spirit can travel while the body is resting, others disagree. Some say that little jump you feel when you are first falling asleep is your spirit jumping back into your body. Others say the spirit of soul can be summoned away from the person and they end up in strange places at night. Some say that feeling of flying is also the spirit or soul traveling. If there is sleep or night travel, it must be of God, else it is self-initiated or demonically initiated and those two mechanisms are not safe.

You pray; you ask the Lord for yourself. I cannot say who goes where or if anyone goes anywhere while their body is at rest. I do know for myself I pray against being summoned so I am not doing something unintentional while I am asleep.

Some describe this night travel as a function of a person who has a very active internal processing system, strong imagery, and unresolved or repeated patterns being worked through. The repetition is not because they are being trapped. It is because something is being repeated without interruption. Repetition is not captivity; it is an unbroken pattern.

If nothing changes in thought, in agreement, or in what is being reinforced, then the same imagery will return. Not because the person is stuck in a realm, but because the pattern has not been interrupted.

If the dreams are frequent, intense, and repetitive, then something needs to be addressed, interrupted, or corrected. You can pray to cancel demonic dreams, you can pray against backward dreams. You can pray to only have Holy Spirit inspired dreams. You can forbid any entities from summoning you and you can command your own soul not to answer evil summons, evil call, or go anywhere that is not of God.

Captivity, in Scripture, is described as a condition, not a location. It is influence, control, or deception. It is being taken captive at one level, and bringing thoughts into captivity at another. The language points to what is operating. However, as discussed repetitive dreams about being lost, especially in a dark forest, wandering, can't find your way back and so forth are indications that your soul is in captivity.

The Bible includes dreams:

- Joseph (Genesis 37) Daniel (Daniel 7)
- Joseph, husband of Mary (Matthew 1–2)

NOTICE, these dreams were initiated by God. They were purposeful, not constant nightly warfare loops. They were not described as traveling to realms, described as getting stuck, described as repeatable on demand. "God speaketh once, yea twice…" (Job 33:14–15). Dreams = communication, not relocation

4. SPIRITUAL WARFARE is real.

We wrestle not against flesh and blood… (Ephesians 6:12) wrestling is conflict, not "traveling to fight in realms". You are not told, "go into another realm and fight."

Immediately I say if you go onto your enemy's turf you have put yourself at extreme disadvantage. Anyone who knows anything about warfare of any kind knows you don't do that unless you have no other recourse.

In the Word we are told to stand, resist, remain

5. AUTHORITY & POSITION

The Word says we are seated… in heavenly places in Christ Jesus, (Ephesians 2:6), This is positional truth, not physical travel or realm visitation. If you go to another realm, your physical body isn't going there anyway, so why try to 'go' there. Just stand where you are and pray. The text says we are "seated in heavenly places in Christ Jesus" and also speaks of "spiritual wickedness in high places." At first glance, this can sound like locations, levels, or places you go.

Heavenly places are not travel destinations. You are not literally instructed to go there, enter them, or move between them. You are described as already seated there. You are not traveling to heavenly places; you are positioned.

What does that mean?

Heavenly places describe spiritual position and authority, not movement or location. It answers where you stand in relation to God, what authority you operate under, and what governs your position.

When Scripture says "seated," it is not describing posture. It is describing authority, rest, and established position. Heavenly places are not where you go; they are where you stand.

At the same time, the text also speaks of spiritual wickedness in high places. So, within the same heavenly context, there is authority in Christ and there is opposition. This tells us that heavenly places describe a dimension of spiritual activity and authority, not a destination. They describe a level of operation, not a place of travel.

If an environment is where something consistently functions, then heavenly places represent the highest level of authority and operation, where Christ rules, believers are positioned, and spiritual conflict is addressed. Heavenly places are not environments you enter. They are the position from which you operate.

You do not ascend into heavenly places. You function from them. This corrects the idea that you must go somewhere to fight, enter something to access power, or travel spiritually to engage. Instead, you stand, you resist, and you remain. Authority is not accessed by movement. It is exercised from position.

Heavenly places are real, spiritual, and authoritative, but they are not scenes, locations you visit, or environments you move through. They are not where you go to get authority. They are where you already have it. You do not travel upward to function. You stand where you have been placed. Movement is not required for authority. Alignment is.

So, I searched. Where in the Bible are people stuck in realms? Not there.

Where do souls travel and get trapped? Not there.

Where did anyone go retrieve someone from a realm? Not there.

Where in the Bible do people fight nightly in other realms? Not described that way.

What is there is captivity (condition) strongholds (patterns) warfare (resistance) dreams (communication) authority (position). Scripture speaks of captivity, strongholds, and resistance— but it does not teach that believers are trapped in realms. The Bible describes **what** holds a person— not a place they have been taken to.

WHAT STANDING DOES

When you do not know where you stand, you will begin to search for where you are not. Standing establishes position, maintains clarity, and refuses confusion. It recognizes that nothing is missing. You are not trying to reach something; you are called to remain where you have been placed.

When everything is brought together, the picture becomes clear. You are not trapped in a realm, traveling through dimensions, or entering environments. You are positioned, responsible, and capable of recognizing what is in operation. You do not need to go anywhere to function. You need to recognize what is already functioning.

What actually changes things is not access, imagination, or experience. It is recognition, interruption, and establishment. You do not change your life by entering something new. You change it by interrupting what should not remain.

The Bible does not teach that you are lost in realms, that you must find your way out, or that you must access something hidden. It teaches clarity, order, authority, and responsibility. You are not searching for position. You have been given one. On deliverance ground and from those who study dreams we have learned to understand more things to help the human condition. God is talking to us all, if we will listen. If we will see patterns, signs, and interpret dreams we can be better informed on how to pray. You are responsible for what you allow to continue. You do not need access. You need alignment.

Stand, and let what is not aligned fall.

When someone comes into your home, they are not given access to everything. They may be welcomed in, but they are not given authority over the entire space. There are rooms they can enter and rooms they cannot, not because the house is divided, but because access is defined.

Presence is not the same as permission. A person can be inside your home, standing in your space, and still not have access to everything within it. Access is not determined by proximity; it is determined by permission.

This is how environments function. Not everything that is present has the right to operate everywhere. There are things that may exist around you, near you, or even within reach, but they do not have to be allowed to function. What is present is not always permitted.

If someone walks into your home and begins to open doors that they were not given access to, that a breach, and it must be addressed. What is not corrected will be repeated. What is not restricted will expand.

An environment is defined by what is allowed to function within it. If something is consistently allowed, it becomes normal. If something is restricted, it cannot establish itself. Permission determines what becomes established.

You are not without control. You may not control everything that exists, but you do determine what is allowed, what is reinforced, and what is refused. Just like your home, you do not chase people through the house or follow them from room to room. You establish where they can be and where they cannot. Authority does not chase. It defines.

You are not at the mercy of everything around you or subject to every influence. You are responsible for what you permit, what you restrict, and what you allow to remain.

Not everything that enters your life has the right to stay, and not everything that stays has the right to operate.

- “What you allow, builds”
- “What you do not interrupt, continues”

WHAT THE BIBLE CALLS A REALM

Heaven and Hell are real—but they are not metaphors. Heaven and Hell can be described as realms. Scripture presents both Heaven and Hell as real, distinct, diametrically opposed to one another, and not interchangeable.

HEAVEN

- "Our Father which art in heaven…" (Matthew 6:9)
- "caught up to the third heaven" (2 Corinthians 12:2)

Heaven is the dwelling place of God. It is a place of authority and order.

HELL

- "the rich man… in hell he lift up his eyes" (Luke 16:23)
- "lake of fire" (Revelation 20:14)

Hell is a place of judgment, separation, and consequence.

These are not environments you drift into, or spaces you accidentally enter, or places you visit and return from.

A realm = *an environment where something consistently functions.*

These are not like other REALMS. They are fixed, defined by God, not shaped by human agreement. Not every realm is formed by people; some are established by God.

The Bible does not teach people traveling between Heaven and Earth at will, people visiting Hell and returning freely, or Believers moving in and out of these realms repeatedly.

Even when someone like Paul references Heaven it was initiated by God, not controlled, not repeatable on demand. What God reveals, He initiates; it is not something man reproduces.

Heaven and hell can be understood as realms in the sense that they are environments with consistent conditions established by God.

Scripture says we can come freely to the Throne of Grace, which means we can present our case, our petition, or ask for our defense from accusations in the Courts of Heaven. There is no requirement or mechanism for humans who are still among the living to teleport to Heaven to meet up with anyone there. Heaven and Hell are not experiences. They are realities established by God. You do not access them. You are appointed to one.

Not every realm is available.

Some are final so since Jesus came and died for us to be free and to be redeemed from eternal death and damnation, we must take advantage of that gracious offer while we still have life in us on this side.

DOORS, BOUNDARIES, AND UNAUTHORIZED ACCESS

A home has structure, not just walls but also doors. Doors define entry, restriction, and control. A door answers one question: *Who is allowed through*?

In your home, some doors are open, some are closed, and some are locked. Each one communicates something different. An open door says access is permitted. A closed door says access is not available. A locked door says access is restricted. A door does not just allow entry. It defines authority.

When boundaries are ignored, the issue is not confusion. If someone enters without permission, opens what was closed, or crosses into restricted space, that is unauthorized access. Unauthorized access is not accidental and it must be challenged.

This kind of access rarely begins in obvious ways. It starts small. A boundary is crossed once and nothing is said. It is crossed again and still nothing is addressed. Over time, what was once restricted becomes familiar, and what becomes familiar becomes accepted. What is repeated without correction becomes permitted.

This is how environments shift. Not through a single event, but through repeated access, unchallenged behavior, and a lack of clear definition. The environment changes because the boundaries changed. When boundaries weaken, environments change.

You do not maintain order by constantly moving or reacting. You establish what is allowed, what is restricted, and what is refused, and you enforce it when necessary. Authority is not constant movement. It is consistent definition.

What I am describing here as environment is not separate from realm. It is the visible expression of it. The realm is the condition. The environment is where that condition is observed. An environment is shaped by what is allowed in, what is kept out, and what is maintained. If access is not controlled, the environment will not remain stable. Uncontrolled access creates unstable environments.

You are not responsible for everything that exists or everything that attempts to enter. But you are responsible for what is allowed to remain and what is permitted to function.

Every environment is defined by its doors, and every door answers to authority. Environments define what surrounds you, permission determines what operates, doors control access, and boundaries maintain what has been established.

DEMAND, CAPACITY, AND AUTHORITY

Not every building receives power the same way.

A residential home receives electricity. It has access, function, and a basic level of supply. But a commercial building operates differently. It is not only supplied; it is measured by demand. Demand is not just usage. It is the capacity to draw, sustain, and handle what is supplied. Supply is available to many, but demand reveals who is built to carry it.

The difference is not the source. Both the home and the commercial building are connected to the same grid. The source is not the issue. The difference is what the structure is authorized and built to handle. The limitation is not in the source. It is in the structure.

This connects directly to how environments function. An environment is where something consistently operates, but what functions depends on capacity, permission, and structure. Some environments can only sustain low demand, minimal flow, and limited operation. Others are built for high demand, sustained flow, and continuous operation. Not every environment is built for the same level of operation.

A residential home is not billed for demand because it is not authorized for that level of draw. Not because power is unavailable, but because the structure is not designed for it. What you are not built to handle, you are not permitted to sustain.

This is where many misunderstand. They assume that if the source is available, they should be able to operate at any level. But that is not how systems work. Access does not equal capacity. Availability does not override design.

In the same way, a person may have access, awareness, and exposure, but not the structure to sustain, maintain, or operate at that level. You can be connected and still not be built for what you are trying to carry.

When capacity does not match demand, systems begin to fail. Circuits trip, or damage occurs. Not because the power is wrong, but because the structure cannot sustain it. Overextension is not expansion. It is misalignment with capacity.

You are not limited by the source. You are shaped by what you are built to handle, what you are authorized to sustain, and what has been established in your environment.

Environments do not just determine what is available. They determine what can be sustained.

YOU DO NOT UPGRADE BY DEMAND—YOU UPGRADE BY BUILD

What works in your realm? At what level? It depends on capacity. You cannot increase capacity by desire, and you cannot sustain more by simply wanting more.

A structure is upgraded through reinforcement, alignment, and consistency. Capacity is not declared; it is developed. When a building is upgraded to handle greater demand, the change is not cosmetic. It requires stronger systems, better distribution, and stable infrastructure. Anything less will fail under pressure. If the structure is not strengthened, increased demand will expose its weakness.

This is where many misstep. They try to access more, do more, and carry more without addressing what is sustaining them, what is reinforcing them, and what is limiting them. So, when pressure increases, failure follows. Not because something is wrong with the source, but because the structure was never upgraded.

Upgrading is not about adding more. It is about correcting what is already there. You do not upgrade a structure by stacking more on top of it. You upgrade it by fixing what is weak, removing what is unstable, and reinforcing what must hold. An upgrade is not addition; it is correction.

If something collapses under pressure, fails when stretched, or cannot hold consistency, that is not a mystery. It is a signal. Something must be strengthened, aligned, or replaced. What fails under pressure reveals what has not been reinforced.

Consistency is what builds capacity. You do not become capable through intensity. You become capable through what you repeat, maintain, and reinforce. Consistency is what turns possibility into capacity.

An environment can support more only if the structure within it can sustain it. If the structure is weak, it will not stabilize at a higher level. Not because it is unavailable, but because it cannot be maintained. You do not rise by access. You rise by what you can sustain.

You are not waiting for more opportunity, more access, or a different environment. You are responsible for what is being built, what is being reinforced, and what is being corrected. That is what determines what you can carry, what you can maintain, and what will remain.

When the structure is ready, what it can carry will change.

What should your realm be like? Simple. Let it be done on Earth as it is in Heaven.

BUT WHO ARE YOU? — AUTHORITY AND AUTHORIZATION

The text says, "Jesus I know, and Paul, I know; but who are ye?" and this moment is not random. It is a revelation. Men attempted to exercise authority that they did not possess. They used the right words, referenced the right name, and performed the right action, but something was missing. Language does not replace authority.

The issue was not the method, the wording, or the intention. It was authorization. They were trying to function in a capacity that had not been established in them. They attempted to operate beyond what they were built and authorized to carry.

This reflects the same structural principle seen elsewhere. Just as a building not designed for high demand cannot sustain that level of draw, these men attempted to access power without structure, without alignment, and without authority, and it failed. Power is not accessed by imitation; it is sustained by authorization.

The response they received is everything. "Jesus, I know. Paul, I know, but who are you?" This is not a conversation. It is recognition. Authority is recognized, even where it is resisted. Jesus was known, and Paul was known because they were aligned, authorized, and established. Their authority was not theoretical. It was functional. Authority is not claimed; it is recognized by what responds.

This is the same principle of unauthorized access. These men, the Sons of Sceva (Acts 19), attempted to enter a space of authority without authorization, and instead of gaining control, they were overpowered. When you operate without authority, you do not establish control; you expose yourself.

They were not in the wrong place or trapped in an environment. They were attempting to operate beyond what had been established in them. The issue was not where they were. It was what they were not.

This is why structure matters. Authority flows from alignment, consistency, and established position, not from language, imitation, or intensity. You cannot function at a level your structure cannot sustain.

The question, "Who are you?" is not about identity alone. It is about recognition of authority. It reveals whether there is alignment, structure, and authorization, or whether there is only repeated language without capacity. If it is not established in you, it will not respond to you. So, you can't always do in your realm what another is doing in their realm, and vice versa.

There is also a difference between repeating something and being recognized in it. Repetition is easy. A person can say the right words, use the right language, and follow the right pattern and still have no authority. Recognition is different. It is not based on what you say or how you say it. It is based on what has been established in you. Repetition imitates. Recognition reveals.

Words can be learned, phrases can be copied, and methods can be repeated, but authority cannot be borrowed. You can repeat what is said, but you cannot repeat what is established.

This is where many are misled. They hear something that works and see someone operating with authority, and they assume that if they do the same thing, they will get the same result. So they repeat it, but nothing responds. Not because the method is wrong, but because the structure is missing. The method may be correct, but without structure, nothing will answer to it.

When something is established, it is recognized. Not because it is declared loudly, but because it is present consistently. What is established does not need to be introduced. It is already known.

Authority is not performance, volume, or repetition. Authority is alignment, consistency, and structure, and it is revealed by what responds. If nothing responds, nothing has been established.

You do not need to repeat more, say it louder, or try again differently. You need to ask what has actually been established, because that determines what recognizes you, what responds to you, and what yields.

You are not recognized for what you repeat. You are recognized for what has been built in you.

WHY EFFORT DOES NOT ALWAYS WORK

Effort is one of the most trusted responses to a lack of results. When something is not working, the natural instinct is to increase effort. Work harder, push further, stay longer, and do more. Effort feels responsible, productive, and like the right response. But effort is not always effective.

There are situations where effort produces results, and there are situations where effort produces exhaustion. The difference is not always the person. The difference is the environment.

Effort works best in environments that support what you are doing. But when you are operating in an environment of resistance, effort becomes strain. You can push and still not move, build and nothing holds, initiate and nothing responds.

This is where frustration begins. The assumption is that if you just do more, something will change. But more effort in the wrong environment does not create breakthrough. It creates fatigue.

This is why some people are tired without progress. Not because they are unwilling, but because they are working in an environment that does not support their output.

One of the most difficult positions to be in is doing the right thing and seeing no results. This creates internal conflict. When something is wrong, it is easier to identify. But when something is right and still not working, it becomes confusing.

A person can make the correct decisions, apply the right principles, and take appropriate action, and still experience resistance. Not because the action is wrong, but because the environment is not aligned with what they are doing. Recall, the environment is not separate from realm. It is the visible expression of it. The realm is the condition. The environment is where that condition is observed.

This is where many begin to question themselves unnecessarily. They assume they misunderstood, missed something, or are not capable. In reality, they are attempting to produce in an environment that does not support their outcome.

The issue is not always correction. Sometimes the issue is relocation. Some people are not failing. They are planted in the wrong environment

DISPLACEMENT BEFORE ESTABLISHMENT

Movement between environments is not always immediate. There is often a period of displacement, a space where what was familiar is no longer functioning, but what is new has not yet stabilized. This can be uncomfortable, because during displacement old patterns stop working, familiar responses lose effectiveness, and nothing feels settled.

Many misinterpret this phase. They assume something is wrong because things are no longer working the way they used to. But sometimes that is the indication that a shift has begun. What once responded no longer does, and what once held no longer remains. This is not always loss. It can be transition.

If a person does not recognize displacement, they will try to return to what is no longer functioning. They will attempt to rebuild in an environment they are no longer supported by, and in doing so, they delay movement.

Movement between environments often requires separation. It is not always dramatic or announced, but it is necessary. You cannot fully function in two conflicting environments at the same time. At some point, there must be distinction. Separation can look like ending a pattern, leaving an environment, changing what you consistently participate in, or refusing to continue what once felt normal.

This is where resistance often increases, because separation disrupts what was previously agreed upon. It interrupts patterns, removes reinforcement, and breaks continuity. What has been established does not release easily. This is why many avoid separation, not because they do not see the need, but because they feel the cost.

Without separation, there is no clear shift, only overlap, and overlap produces confusion.

A person can experience a moment of change and assume the environment has shifted, but moments do not establish environments. Consistency does. A decision can initiate movement, but it must be reinforced. If what created the previous environment is still in place, that environment will reassert itself.

This is why people return to patterns they thought they left, not because they intended to go back, but because the environment was never fully changed.

An environment has shifted when what used to work no longer does, what used to resist begins to respond, and what required force becomes natural. This is not emotional. It is observable. You will not have to convince yourself something has changed. You will see it in what is now supported.

YOU CANNOT FORCE A REALM TO RESPOND

This is where many exhaust themselves. They attempt to force results in an environment that does not support them. They push harder. They insist longer. They apply pressure repeatedly. A realm does not respond to pressure. It responds to alignment. Force can produce temporary movement.

It does not create stability. What is forced must be maintained by force. What is aligned sustains itself. **You don't need more effort. You need a different realm.**

Recognizing when it is time to move. There comes a point where continued effort is no longer productive, and persistence is no longer wisdom. This is not quitting. This is recognition.

When nothing is holding, nothing is responding, and everything requires strain, it is time to evaluate the environment, not just the action or the method. Staying in the wrong environment does not produce breakthrough; it produces wear, frustration, exhaustion, and defeat.

Movement requires decision. An environment does not shift accidentally. At some point, there must be a decision to stop reinforcing what is not working, to interrupt what has been allowed, and to disengage from what sustains the current environment.

This is where movement begins, not in emotion and not in effort, but in decision followed by consistency.

When two realms occupy the same space

Not every environment is unified. Some spaces are shared physically but divided operationally. Two people can stand in the same room and be functioning under completely different conditions. One experiences access while the other experiences resistance. One moves with ease while the other struggles for the same outcome. This is not always about skill or effort. It is often about the environment they are operating from.

An environment is not limited by physical boundaries. It is carried, sustained, and operates wherever its conditions are maintained. When two individuals enter the same space, they do not automatically enter the same environment. They bring with them what they have been functioning in.

Sometimes, those environments collide.

WHY THINGS WORK FOR ONE PERSON AND NOT ANOTHER

This is one of the most misunderstood realities. Two people can use the same method, follow the same process, and apply the same principles, yet produce completely different results. This is where comparison becomes dangerous. Without understanding environments, the assumption is that the difference must be intelligence, effort, favor, or timing. But sometimes the difference is environment.

One person is functioning in a setting that supports the outcome. The other is functioning in a setting that resists it. So one builds and it holds. The other builds and it collapses. Not because one is right and the other is wrong, but because one is supported and the other is not. You can copy a method, but you cannot copy the environment that sustains it.

When someone carries a different environment into a space, the results can appear unusual. Things begin to happen that are not typical for that setting. Doors open that normally remain closed. Progress occurs where stagnation is expected. Movement happens where delay is the norm.

This is often misunderstood. People may attribute it to personality, luck, or exception. But what is actually happening is that a different environment has entered the space, and for a time it overrides what is normal there. Proximity, agreement, and what actually transfers.

There are environments where certain outcomes are common. In some places, opportunity circulates, expectation is high, and results repeat. This is not always a matter of individual ability. It is often the result of collective agreement about what is normal. What a group expects consistently, it tends to produce repeatedly.

This is why people move toward rooms where things happen, networks where access is normal, and circles where outcomes are common. They are not just chasing people. They are trying to enter an environment of different expectations. People do not just seek people. They seek the environment those people operate in.

However, this needs correction. Proximity can expose you, stretch you, and recalibrate what you think is possible, but it does not transfer structure, install discipline, or establish capacity. Access can open your eyes, but it cannot build your structure.

What actually transfers from those environments is perspective, language, standards, and expectation. These things matter because they can raise what you believe is normal. Exposure can raise expectation, but only structure can sustain results.

Some people change and others do not. Two people can enter the same room, and one will observe, adjust, and build while the other will visit, admire, and leave unchanged. The proximity is the same, but the outcome is different. The room can influence you, but it cannot build you.

Collective agreement creates shared expectations, shared standards, and repeated outcomes. This is why some places feel like things just work there, while others feel like nothing ever moves. Agreement sets the baseline for what is expected to happen. People may go to those spaces hoping to enter a better environment, but you do not change environments by proximity alone. You change by what you adopt, what you reinforce, and what you maintain.

You can visit a higher environment and remain unchanged, or you can adopt its standards and become established. Proximity may introduce you, but structure determines whether you remain.

This is why some people change environments without trying. There are individuals who enter a space and things begin to shift. That person didn't announce change or force anything. It could be that what they carry alters what is tolerated. Patterns begin to break. New results begin to appear. What was once stable becomes disrupted. This is not always welcomed because established realms do not yield easily.

Sometimes what enters is not aligned with what should be established in a given space. This is where *unauthorized access* occurs. Something begins to function in an environment where it was not originally present. At first, it may seem small, unnoticeable, even insignificant or easy to ignore. But if it is not addressed… it begins to establish itself. Through repetition. Through tolerance. Through lack of interruption. over time… what was once foreign… becomes normal.

Realm collisions create tension. When two conflicting environments are present, tension is unavoidable, because what one supports, the other resists. This tension often appears as inconsistency, instability, sudden shifts in outcomes, or unpredictable results. Things work one moment and fail the next. Progress appears and then disappears. Clarity is present, and then confusion follows. This is not randomness. It is collision.

When environments are not aligned, stability cannot be maintained because there is no unified condition. Different forces are operating at the same time, different patterns are being reinforced, and different outcomes are being produced. Without alignment, nothing holds consistently. This is why some spaces feel unsettled, unpredictable, or difficult to sustain progress in. It is not because nothing is working, but because too many things are operating at once.

One of the clearest signs of this kind of collision is that you can be present in a space, and nothing responds to you. You have access to the environment but no support within it. You can participate, but not produce. This is where many become frustrated, because from the outside it appears that everything is available, but from within nothing is cooperating. You can be present in a place and still be operating from a different environment.

WHEN REALMS DO NOT ALIGN, ONE WILL DOMINATE

Environments do not coexist equally forever. Over time, one will become dominant. The one that is reinforced, maintained, and allowed will define what surrounds you. This is why passive agreement is dangerous. What is not resisted is reinforced, and what is reinforced becomes established.

This is why discernment is necessary. Without it, collisions between environments are misinterpreted. People begin to assume that inconsistency is normal, instability is expected, and unpredictability is unavoidable. But these are often signs of misalignment, and until that misalignment is recognized, nothing will stabilize.

You cannot build consistently in a colliding environment. Progress requires stability, and stability requires alignment. If conditions are in conflict, what you build will not hold. Not because it is wrong, but because the environment cannot sustain it.

This is where many become discouraged. They are building correctly in an unstable environment, and what is built in instability must constantly be rebuilt.

Where environments collide, consistency dies.

A REALM DOES NOT ESTABLISH ITSELF BY ACCIDENT

If an environment can be formed unintentionally, it can also be established intentionally. But intention alone is not enough. An environment is not built by desire, and it is not sustained by occasional effort. It is established through what is consistently permitted, reinforced, and maintained.

Many want a different environment, but they do not change what they allow, but what is allowed will always rebuild what was there before, like a perennial plant if it's good, or a weed, if it is bad.

Before anything new can be established, something must be removed. Not everything can coexist, and not everything can remain. If confusion is present, clarity cannot stabilize. If lack is reinforced, provision will not hold. If resistance is active, progress will not sustain.

This is where many hesitate, because removal feels like loss. Patterns must be interrupted. Access must be restricted. Participation must be reconsidered. This is not punishment; it is preparation. What is removed creates space, and what fills that space will define what comes next.

Removal alone does not establish an environment. It creates absence, but absence is not structure. Something must replace what was removed, and that replacement must be reinforced.

Reinforcement looks like consistency, repetition, and a refusal to return to what was removed. An environment begins to stabilize, not instantly, but in pattern. What is done once introduces possibility. What is done repeatedly establishes what becomes normal.

Every environment requires maintenance. Not because it is weak, but because it is responsive. It responds to what is present. If what established it is no longer maintained, something else will begin to take its place. As you know, environment is not separate from realm. It is the visible expression of it. The realm is the condition. The environment is where that condition is observed.

This is where many lose what they built. Not because it failed, but because it was not maintained. Maintenance is not dramatic; it is consistent. It is continuing what works, interrupting what does not, and refusing what attempts to re-enter.

If you do not maintain what has been established, it will default to the strongest influence present.

REALMS RESPOND TO CONSISTENCY, NOT INTENSITY

Many try to establish change through intensity. They apply pressure, make strong decisions, and create powerful moments. Intensity does not sustain an environment. Consistency does. A single strong moment cannot override a sustained pattern, but a sustained pattern will eventually override everything else. This is why small, consistent actions carry more weight than occasional intensity, because environments respond to what is repeated.

Once something is properly established, it begins to function without strain. What once required effort begins to respond naturally. This is where things shift. You are no longer pushing constantly, forcing outcomes, or trying to hold everything together. The environment begins to support what you are doing.

This is the difference between maintaining results and sustaining an environment. Results must be managed. An environment produces.

What is established must also be protected. Not everything should have access, and not everything should be allowed to interact freely with what has been built. Access influences environment. If something enters that contradicts what has been established, it begins to weaken it. Not immediately, but gradually.

This is why boundaries are necessary—not as restriction, but as preservation.

A realm will reveal whether it is stable. You will know a realm is established when what used to disrupt no longer affects it. what used to require effort becomes natural. what once resisted now responds. You will know when what is around you is not temporary, but sustained, repeatable, consistent if not constant. You will not have to convince yourself it is working. You will see it in what consistently holds.

This is where control returns. When you understand realms, you stop reacting to outcomes… …and start governing environments. You stop asking, "Why is this not working?" Instead, you will ask, "What is in operation here?" That question changes everything. Because once you identify what is in operation…you can decide whether it remains.

You are not just managing results. You are establishing what is allowed to exist around you.

can he be in one realm and she is in another and that is a relationship thorn or disconnect? Yes, that's **real.** a man can be functioning in one realm, and a woman in another… and the issue is not always compatibility.

It is **misaligned environments**.

Two people can be connected…dating, even married…and not be functioning in the same realm. One may be in a realm of clarity. The other in a realm of confusion. One may be moving with consistency, the other with instability.

Both can be sincere, both can care and be trying. But sincerity does not override environment. This is where disconnect forms. Not always because something is wrong with either person……but because what supports one…is resisted in the other.

Connection does not guarantee alignment. You can love someone… and still not be able to function with them—because you are not operating in the same realm.

Discern what is actually happening.

NOT EVERY "REALM" IS A REALM

There are many who use the word "realm" to describe experiences that are not actually realms. Some speak of opening realms, accessing realms, or moving through realms to gain information. Not everything labeled a realm is an environment of operation.

A realm is not a mental space. It is not imagination, thought, or internal visualization. It is not something you enter by thinking, and it is not something you open by intention alone. A realm is revealed by what consistently functions around you. If it does not produce consistent outcomes, it is not a realm; it is an experience.

A realm is also not information access. Some use the language of realms to describe how they access knowledge. They say they opened a realm and got the answer, or entered a realm of understanding. Access to information is not the same as functioning within an environment. You can think clearly, remember quickly, or process information efficiently and still not be operating in a different realm. Information can be accessed internally, but a realm is experienced externally through what responds.

A realm does not require imagination to enter. You do not imagine your way into a realm; you recognize it by what is already happening. If something must be maintained by visualization, emotional intensity, or mental effort, then it is not a realm. It is a constructed experience. A realm does not depend on your focus to exist. It continues whether you acknowledge it or not.

This distinction matters. If everything is called a realm, nothing is clearly understood. You will begin to chase experiences, mislabel processes, and misunderstand what is actually affecting your life. Instead of recognizing what is in operation, you will try to create what is not.

A realm is not defined by what you feel. It is defined by what consistently functions. It determines what works, what fails, what grows, and what resists you. You do not open a realm to get answers. You recognize a realm by what answers to you.

Not everything you feel is something you are in. There are experiences, and there are environments, and they are not the same.

An experience is temporary, internal, and often influenced by emotion, thought, or perception. An environment is sustained, external in its effects, and consistent in what it produces. You can have an experience that feels powerful and yet produces nothing. You can feel clarity in a moment, confidence for a season, or insight during reflection and still return to the same outcomes.

Why?

Because experience does not establish environment. An experience can feel real, but an environment produces results.

This is where many are misled. They have an experience and assume something has changed. They feel breakthrough, release, or understanding, but when they return to their daily life, nothing responds differently. Because what they experienced did not alter what was in operation. If nothing responds differently, nothing has been established.

Environments do not fluctuate with feeling. An environment does not change because of a moment. It changes because of what is interrupted, replaced, and maintained. This is why consistency matters more than intensity. Intensity creates experiences, but consistency establishes environments.

You are not responsible for every experience you have, but you are responsible for what you allow to become your environment. That is determined over time by what you continue, what you reinforce, and what you refuse to interrupt.

Do not mistake what you felt for what has been established.

PARALLEL REALMS

Not everything that feels like change is change. There are moments when something feels different. You may feel lighter, clearer, or more resolved, but *feeling* different is not the same as functioning differently.

Change is not measured by a moment. A moment can inspire, reveal, or expose, but it does not establish an environment. What is established is revealed over time by what continues. Change is not proven by what you felt; it is proven by what continues to respond.

When something has truly changed, what used to resist begins to respond, what used to delay begins to move, and what used to collapse begins to hold. You will not have to convince yourself. You will see it in what now functions.

If, after a moment, the same patterns return, the same resistance remains, and the same outcomes repeat, then nothing has been established. Something may have been revealed, but it has not yet been reinforced. Revelation shows you what is possible. Establishment determines what remains.

This is where many stop too early. They recognize, feel, and understand, but they do not interrupt, replace, and maintain. So, the environment remains unchanged.

Real change requires participation. You do not create change by observation alone. You create it by what you do next. What you continue, what you remove, what you reinforce, and what you refuse—that is what determines what actually changes.

What you do after you see determines what will remain.

An environment does not shift because you noticed it. It shifts when what sustained it is no longer allowed, and when something else is consistently established in its place.

Until what sustained it is interrupted, nothing has changed. Until something new is maintained, nothing will.

Is it the relationship between realms and time, realms and captivity, realms and relationships (people), or something else you were about to connect?

Sometimes people mix time, realms, experience, and imagination, going all sci-fi. We see videos online all the time about people who time travel or believe they do. Just because it *sounds deep doesn't mean it is deep or even true.*

- Some believe they got stuck in the future, or the past.
- Some believe that there are parallel realms.
- Some believe they have moved ahead of time.

They are usually describing one of three things:

1. MENTAL PROJECTION (most common)

A person is imagining scenarios, anticipating outcomes, rehearsing possibilities. Their mind is operating in *"what could happen"* Translation: They are not in the future; they are thinking ahead.

2. EMOTIONAL DISPLACEMENT

Sometimes people are anxious about what's coming overwhelmed by possibilities, mentally living in "later" instead of "now." They are not in another realm. They are not present in their current moment.

3. PATTERN AWARENESS (this one feels supernatural). Some people can see outcomes early, recognize trajectories, predict what's likely. So it *feels like*: they've "seen the future." Translation: they recognized the pattern before others did.

This comes mostly from physics ideas (multiverse theory) sci-fi language spiritualized imagination. A realm is an environment where certain outcomes are consistently produced This is not about *alternate timelines,* duplicate versions of reality, or branching universes you step into. This is universes language.

What is the relationship between realms and time? Time does not create realms. However, realms govern how time is experienced. Time is constant. But how time behaves in your life…is not. In one environment things move quickly, results come together, delays are minimal.

In another everything slows down. progress drags. nothing aligns. You are not in a different time. You are in a different environment affecting how time responds.

WHY PEOPLE FEEL "OUT OF TIME" When someone says "I feel ahead" "I feel behind" "I feel stuck," they are experiencing misalignment between themselves and their current realm. Not time travel, future displacement, parallel existence. Feeling out of time is often being out of alignment.

YOU ARE NOT IN ANOTHER TIME. You are not in the future. You are not in a parallel version of your life. You are not stuck in a different timeline. You are in an environment… that is affecting how things move, how they respond, and how long things take.

Time is not trapping you. Something is governing how it is working around you. People use language like realms, timelines, dimensions to describe something they cannot explain.

But what they are often experiencing is environment + pattern + perception. Realms → environments. Time → consistent, but experienced differently. “Stuck” → sustained resistance or misalignment.

You are not moving through different timelines. You are experiencing different responses within the same time.

WHAT "OPENING A PORTAL" USUALLY MEANS

When someone says, "I open a portal and enter a realm to get information," they are almost always describing a shift in state, not a doorway. In reality, what is happening is a rapid shift into deep focus—a change in the way the mind operates rather than a literal entrance into a new space. This experience is not about crossing a physical boundary but about transitioning into a mental state where information becomes accessible. The individual has learned to move quickly from being scattered to concentrated, from surface thinking to deep processing.

For many, it can feel like stepping "into" something entirely different. They've mastered the art of switching cognitive modes, moving from verbal to visual thinking, from linear to associative patterns, and from conscious reasoning to intuitive processing. To the person, this shift feels like crossing a boundary—almost as if their mind changes gears very fast. The vivid language used to describe this process often serves to impress or convey a sense of control, but it is essentially a way of describing an internal experience.

Terms like portal, realm, and dimension are frequently employed to articulate these experiences. They are often used to capture the feeling of being able to get into one's best thinking mode on demand. However, this is not the same as the formal definition of a realm. While a portal suggests entry into a place, in this framework, there is no actual need for portals. You don't enter realms by opening something; instead, realms are environments of operation that exist independently of whether or not you engage them.

The idea that you must open a portal to access a realm can be misleading. If you have to open, sustain, or imagine a state for it to exist, then it is dependent on you—it is not a realm, but rather an experience. Realms are not accessed by technique; they are revealed by what consistently responds, resists, and continues in your environment. This distinction is crucial, as it clarifies that what many describe as "opening a portal" is actually a shift in state, not movement into a new place.

People often chase experiences, believing they must open, access, or enter something to achieve new outcomes. In doing so, they may overlook what is already governing their results. Chasing access can distract from recognizing what is already in operation. Realms are not accessed by technique; they are revealed by the ongoing reality of response and resistance.

Not everything that sounds like access is movement. When someone claims to "open a realm," what they are most likely describing is a trained or natural ability to access information quickly, combined with metaphorical or inflated language. It is not literal realm navigation or actual movement into knowledge spaces, but rather an internal process—deep focus, pattern recognition, and intuitive thinking.

Some people say they open realms to retrieve information, but realms are for producing outcomes, not simply for accessing knowledge. Ultimately, realms are environments of consistent operation, not mystical access points or knowledge compartments. They are not something you open to get information; instead, they are recognized by what is already functioning where you are.

Folks, there are familiar *spirits* just waiting for someone to 'access a portal' so they can start lying to them. This is what divination is all about. Some of the information may be true to rope the person in, but count on most of it being lies. Still, it is to tie the person to that entity and get a connection going, to get worship out of the human and then take over and begin to control that person. After that, you want to talk about anchor babies or family migration, they will bring in all kinds of other demons and before a person knows it they are inundated by evil spiritual entities. Nothing is free in the dark kingdom.

FLOOR LIMIT AUTHORITY

A realm is where you function consistently what responds to you without strain. It is what operates within your established authority and capacity, where you live, exist, abide, dwell not just physically. It's where you function, where things respond, where patterns are stable.

A realm is not just where you are, it is what consistently works around you. It is what works where you go providing another stronger realm is not greater than yours, as discussed in colliding realms. In certain systems, there is a limit of authority. A banker can approve up to a certain amount… without asking anyone else. That is called a floor limit. Within that limit decisions are immediate. approval is automatic, no escalation is required

Within a defined limit, authority operates without resistance. God is trusting you to establish your own realm, and your capacity establishes your floor limit. Your realm is created simply by what you allow or disallow, consistently. That is done by your actions as well as your words. You must even consider your thought life as thoughts are part of the imagination and they can express desires and invite outcomes.

Now, regarding capacity, what happens above the limit? Once something exceeds that level it must be reviewed and it must be escalated. The desired outcome may be delayed or denied, not because it is impossible, but because it is outside the current level of authority What exceeds your established authority will not respond automatically.

A realm functions like a limit.

Within what has been established, things respond, decisions resolve, and movement happens. This is not because it is easy, but because it is within your capacity and authority. What is within your realm responds without escalation.

When something is outside what has been established, it resists, it delays, and it requires more than you currently sustain. This is not because it is unavailable, but because it has not yet been established within your structure. Resistance often indicates you are operating beyond what has been established.

A realm is shaped by what has been established, what has been reinforced, and what can be sustained. Grace and favor may open opportunities, but authority and capacity determine what holds. Grace may open the door, but capacity determines what remains.

A realm is the level at which things respond to you without escalation. A realm is the environment where your authority, capacity, and consistency produce stable outcomes.

Where you must constantly escalate, you are outside your established realm. Where things respond, you are within it. That would warn people about trying to operate above their "floor limit."

Floor limit means that everything you ask is approved. Whatever you ask, as long as the person is *abiding* and the request is an abiding request, then the answer is Yes, and Amen.

> If ye abide in me, and my words abide in you, ye shall ask what ye will, and it shall be done unto you. (John 15:7)

This is not a blank check; it is a defined condition. The condition is *abiding* which is not occasional agreement, momentary alignment, or selective obedience. Abiding is continuous, consistent, and established. It means you remain you are shaped; you are governed. Abiding is not visiting; it is remaining. *Abiding* is not flossing your teeth on your dental appointment day; it is flossing daily.

When a person abides their thinking aligns, their desires are formed. their requests are shaped. So what they ask… is no longer independent. It is in alignment with what is already established. An abiding request is not separate from alignment; it is produced by it. Within that abiding state there is no escalation because the request, the alignment, and the authority are already in agreement.

Abiding establishes a realm where response does not require escalation. This is the true "everything" "Whatever you ask" is anything that flows from abiding alignment. Everything does not mean anything, it means anything that remains within what has been established. Without abiding, requests conflict. desires divide, and outcomes do not hold. With abiding requests there is alignment. Authority is recognized, and response is consistent.

The promise is not in asking; it is in abiding. Within this the “floor limit” is not partial, it is complete within the boundary of abiding. This does not mean instant gratification, or control over outcomes. It does mean alignment produces consistent favorable response.

Abiding is the structure. The Word is the reinforcement. The request is the expression; the response is the result.

The floor limit of abiding is not partial, it is complete within alignment. You do not ask outside of abiding and expect response; you ask from within it.

Misaligned requests are why people *ask and don't receive* without breaking your tone.

Ring. Ring. "I'm sorry, the realm you have requested is out of the coverage area. Please check your *abiding* or dial again. Click. That is what happens when the request is made but the alignment is not present. It is not that the answer is denied. The request is not recognized.

You can dial the number. You can say the words. You can repeat the request, but if the line is not active… nothing will connect. Repetition does not create connection. Volume doesn’t create connection. Crying doesn’t create connection; alignment does.

Abiding keeps the line open. Without it requests disconnect, responses do not come, and nothing holds

Abiding is not what you do after the request. It is what makes the request valid. Before you dial again… check what you're abiding in.

A signal only works within range, within structure, within connection. Outside of that, the call drops. the signal weakens, or nothing connects at all. Connection requires alignment. Range is determined by structure. A realm defines your operational range.

Within it, things respond, movement happens, requests connect. Outside of it resistance increases, delay appears, or nothing holds. Where there is no response, you may be outside your established range.

Abiding is what stabilizes connection, extends capacity, and maintains range. Without it, you are attempting to operate beyond what is currently sustained. Abiding does not just connect you, it extends what you can carry. Before you dial again… make sure you're in range.

When people get 'refused,' this when they go and get someone else, a supposed higher up to alley-oop their prayer request. This can be how a person can receive something, say healing IN a prayer service and get home and not still be 'healed.' The church and service and corporate anointing was a whole different realm than their prayerless dry house. No, I'm not calling anyone a fake, but maintain your deliverance and your healing by creating a Godly realm and upgrading your capacity in the disciplines of the faith, especially in prayer, decrees, and declarations.

The words that come out of your mouth, especially in your home, are far more powerful than many people realize.

What you allow to play over the airwaves in your home has impact. As said before, what you allow and disallow in yourself and your own life -- , even your thoughts – the meditations of your heart help create your realm.

There is nothing wrong with seeking someone to pray with you or for you. Scripture says that there *are* moments where someone's faith helps another. The friends who brought the paralytic to Jesus, (Mark 2:3–5). Jesus saw their faith. Notice: they brought him to Jesus they did not replace his own relationship with Jesus. You can benefit from someone else's faith, someone else's agreement, someone else's clarity. We can ask the Elders of the church to pray for us. In agreement with two or three others, words can be established. Additionally, we are supposed to pray for one another. Amen.

You cannot permanently operate on someone else's structure. Agreement can assist you, but it cannot replace what must be established in you. There are times when people feel weak, unsure, or disconnected, so they go to someone who feels strong, confident, or anointed. And something does happen. But the misunderstanding is thinking that person is a permanent higher access point. Help can carry you into something, but it cannot maintain it for you.

This becomes especially clear when asking why people receive something in one setting and do not retain it in another. In a corporate environment, faith is high, agreement is strong, and focus is clear. That environment helps a person receive. But receiving and maintaining are not the same. What you receive in a moment must be sustained in your life.

An environment can help you receive, but your life must sustain what was received. If nothing changes around what was received, it may not remain. This does not mean the moment was false. It means that maintenance matters. Continuation is what stabilizes what has been received. Someone can help you receive, but they cannot live it for you. A moment can open the door, but what surrounds you determines what stays.

This principle becomes very clear in everyday life. A person can spend a year in the gym, disciplined, consistent, and focused. They become fit, strong, and defined, not by accident, but by what they consistently did. Then something changes, not their body first, but their environment. The workouts slow down, the structure loosens, and a new pattern begins. The snacks increase, the discipline fades, and the consistency breaks. The body did not change first. The environment did.

Nothing dramatic happened overnight, but what was reinforced changed. Over time, what was built began to reverse. Not because the gym stopped working, but because the person stopped remaining in what built it. What built you must be maintained, or it will be undone.

This is not a mystery. The gym works, and the snacks work too. Both produce consistent results. The question is not what works, but what you are remaining in. Every environment produces something, and you will reflect what you remain in.

An environment is not complicated. It is simply what you consistently participate in, what you reinforce, and what you maintain. Change the pattern, and the outcome follows. You do not lose results randomly. You leave what produced them.

You do not have to guess, wonder, or overthink. Look at what is being repeated. That will tell you what environment you are in. If you want to know what is producing your life, look at what you have been consistently allowing.

This same principle shows up in relationships. There are things that begin well because effort is high, attention is focused, and consistency is present. As a result, something responds, whether it is a relationship, a result, or a change. But over time, what produced it is reduced. The effort drops, attention shifts, and consistency breaks, and what was gained begins to weaken.

What you did to establish it is what sustains it. If something responded to consistency, attention, and effort, it will require those same things to remain. You do not keep what you stop maintaining.

The shift many miss is that they want continued results without continued reinforcement. They ask what changed, but the answer is simple. What was being done stopped being done. When the pattern changes, the outcome follows.

If you want greater results, stronger outcomes, or increased stability, you cannot remain at the same level of input. Expansion requires reinforcement, not assumption. An environment does not sustain itself. It is sustained by what is repeated, what is reinforced, and what is maintained. If you want to keep it, keep doing what built it. If you want more, build stronger.

WHAT TYPE OF SPIRITUAL AUTHORITY GOVERNS A REALM?

When considering what governs a realm, many wonder if it is a territorial power, a principality, or whether tension and warfare between good and bad forces are at play. This is an important question—and it's precisely where people can move from clear, practical truth into speculation if they aren't careful. To avoid confusion, it's best to keep the discussion biblical, straightforward, and consistent.

Scripture acknowledges layers of spiritual opposition. Ephesians 6:12 references "principalities… powers… rulers of the darkness… spiritual wickedness in high places," indicating various spiritual authorities exist. However, the Bible does not lay them out as territories on a grid, named regions you track, or realms you travel through. Instead, it affirms spiritual authority without instructing believers to map it out in detail.

So, what governs what you experience? Rather than asking, "Which spirit governs this realm?", it is wiser to ask, "What is consistently being allowed and reinforced here?" In Scripture, outcomes are closely tied to agreement, alignment, obedience or disobedience, and what is practiced and continued. What is established and maintained is what governs a realm.

TERRITORIAL *spirits*

People often say, "this city has a *spirit* over it," or "this region is controlled by…" While Scripture hints at regional influence (such as Daniel 10's reference to the "prince of the kingdom of Persia"), it does not instruct believers to map territories, identify ruling *spirits* over locations, or engage them by name. Influence may exist, but the Believer's responsibility is to align with God's Truth.

IS THERE WARFARE?

The Bible says, "Resist the devil, and he will flee from you" (James 4:7). Warfare is about resistance and standing firm. Having done all to stand therefore in your authority.

GOOD VS BAD REALMS?

Scripture frames environments as light vs darkness, truth vs deception, and obedience vs disobedience. What aligns with God produces order. A realm, by definition, is an environment where something consistently functions. What governs it is what is consistently practiced, permitted, reinforced, and maintained. You don't need to name what governs it to see what is governing it.

There is opposition, influence, and resistance, but it is spiritually dangerous for the Believer, on their own, individually to chase, or engage spiritual geographical forces. The Archangel Michael had to come to help Daniel and I suspect Daniel had a tight realm, ample capacity, full authority in his jurisdiction. Principalities and even territorial spirits are nothing to play with. Instead, Believers are called to stand, align, resist, and remain. You change your environment by what you establish within it. What you reinforce will govern what surrounds you.

LIFE AND DEATH ARE IN THE POWER OF THE TONGUE.

Those who love to talk, those who love to say a lot of words will enjoy the fruit of those words. Your own words could be governing your realm. More than once in the Bible people got exactly what they said, even though they wanted those results for others. So remember vengeance is the Lords, and it would be better to be quiet than to say something that will backfire on yourself.

SPIRITUAL MAPPING

Spiritual mapping—such as tracking family lines, regional *spirits*, or identifying what's over a territory—is common practice. The main scriptural reference is Daniel 10:13, which speaks of the "prince of the kingdom of Persia." This illustrates spiritual resistance connected to a region, but Daniel did confront it directly himself, or build a system around identifying it. Scripture reveals influence but does not assign Believers the task of mapping it.

YOU HAVE TO CALL A DEMON BY NAME

Many people practice spiritual mapping and naming *spirits*, some say you don't need to name *spirits* that are operating, others say you do. They say you do because if you don't call them by name they don't answer or respond to your commands.

This idea is often tested against Mark 5:9, where Jesus asks the demon for its name ("Legion"). Yet, Jesus was not dependent on the name to exercise authority. In other examples, such as Luke 4:35 and Matthew 8:16, Jesus simply commanded *spirits* to leave without naming or identifying them. Scripture shows that authority is not dependent on identification; power is in authority, not in naming.

While knowing a name can be helpful at times, it is not required. Practices like spiritual mapping and naming *spirits* often feel strategic and thorough, but they can overcomplicate, distract, and shift focus away from alignment. Complexity can feel like power—even when it replaces true authority.

You don't have to identify everything influencing a situation to change what is operating. Your responsibility is not to map every influence. Authority does not require a name to function. If authority depends on identification, it is no longer authority—it becomes a method. Over-analysis and unnecessary complexity distract from your true assignment.

When authority waits for identification, it has already been reduced. You don't need to call it "this spirit," "that entity," or "this category." You can address what is happening without naming everything. Authority does not begin with identification. Clarity may help you see it, but authority is what changes it. You are not waiting to define everything; you are responsible for what you allow to continue.

Whether named or unnamed, pronounced correctly or not at all, authority is not in what you call it. It is in the position and alignment you hold. You are not stalled by the precision of language or by whether you have the exact name. You operate from position, not technique. Named or unnamed—whosoever, whatsoever, *whatchamacallit*—authority is not in what you call it.

REALMS MISMATCH

When You Are Judged by the Wrong Environment

There are things that do not fail. They are simply placed where they cannot function. A seed in concrete is not a bad seed; it is a misplaced one. Many people have spent years correcting themselves, when the issue was never correction. It was placement.

Mismatch is when something valid is placed in an environment that cannot read it, hold it, or respond to it correctly. Instead of adjusting the environment, the environment judges the thing.

Is it possible to be not enough and too much at the same time? Yes. That is not confusion. That is a diagnosis. You are too much for what cannot manage you, and not enough for what cannot define you.

Every environment operates by its own conditions. Different settings produce different outcomes. Nothing is wrong in itself, but things are not interchangeable. When you are placed in the wrong environment, your function is misread, your value is reduced, and your output is questioned.

There are several ways mismatch reveals itself. In a capacity mismatch, what you carry exceeds what the environment can handle. As a result, it is delayed, dismissed, or downplayed—not because it is incorrect, but because it is beyond what can be sustained there. In a control mismatch, your presence disrupts the need for control. Even without speaking, you introduce thought, perspective, and alternative. That alone is enough to trigger rejection.

In a presentation mismatch, what is valued is loud, visible, and performative, while what you carry is structured, contained, and weighty. It is overlooked, not because it lacks value, but because it is not recognized in that form. In a timing mismatch, you arrive before the environment is ready. Early things are often rejected, mocked, or ignored, only to be adopted later when the environment has shifted.

At its core, mismatch is a placement issue. You can be functioning correctly and still be in the wrong environment.

A person who does not understand mismatch will begin to shrink themselves, overexplain themselves, or perform to gain acceptance. They attempt to make an environment accept what it was never built to receive. This is where unnecessary correction begins—adjusting what was never wrong.

Mismatch is not failure. It is misplacement.

A mismatch occurs when something valid is placed in the wrong environment, and the thing itself becomes labeled as too much, not enough, unnecessary, or difficult. The signs are consistent. You are constantly being adjusted but never received. Your input is ignored, then later adopted elsewhere. You feel both overqualified and undervalued at the same time. What you carry works—but not there.

A capacity mismatch reveals an environment that cannot recognize or steward what is present. A control mismatch exposes resistance to anything that cannot be contained. A realm mismatch shows that different environments produce different outcomes, and what works in one will not function in another. A presentation mismatch reflects a difference in what is valued and what is recognized. A timing mismatch reveals that arrival and readiness are not always aligned.

The danger of mismatch is not the environment itself, but the response to it. Without discernment, a person may shrink what is correct, silence what is needed, or overperform to compensate. They attempt to fit a place that was never built for them.

Mismatch reveals two things: what you carry, and where it belongs—by where it does not work.

You do not fix mismatch by becoming less, explaining more, or performing differently. You fix mismatch by placement.

People who have been misread, mislabeled, and misplaced do not need to become something else. They need to be positioned where what they carry is understood.

GOD GAVE EARTH TO MAN

The heaven, even the heavens, are the Lord's: but the earth hath he given to the children of men. (Psalm 115:16)

God gave the Earth to man.

We, as the sons of God (or prophetically as the sons of God) are supposed to be establishing, stewarding, co-creating with God, or doing our part in the Earth under God's authority. We, as sons of God are supposed to be establishing what works here, in the Earth, and what doesn't. What should be setting parameters as to what is allowed here-- what isn't.

Thy kingdom come. Thy will be done in earth, as *it is* in heaven. (Matthew 6:10)

We are supposed to be exercising authority and say-so over what this realm is supposed to create, allow, produce. If we don't some other force will try to dictate the properties and conditions of this Earth Realm. So, this realm affects us but we, in proper authority should be affecting the Realm.

The Earth is a governed realm. Scripture shows that God gave the Earth to man, not for passive existence, but for stewardship, responsibility, and function. We, as the sons of God, are not meant to simply exist within this realm. We are meant to establish, steward, and operate under God's authority within it.

This means that what functions here is not supposed to be random. It is not supposed to be left undefined. It is not supposed to be dictated by whatever force happens to assert itself. The responsibility of defining what is allowed, what is not, what produces, and what is restrained has been given to those who are aligned with God's authority; the sons of God on assignment here in the Earth.

The Earth responds to what is established within it. It reflects what is permitted, what is reinforced, and what is maintained. This is why the realm can affect people, but it is not supposed to govern them without response. Properly aligned authority is meant to influence the realm, not be shaped by it without resistance.

When that responsibility is not exercised, something else will attempt to define the conditions. If what should be established is left unestablished, then what should not be present will begin to take root. The environment will not remain neutral. It will respond to whatever is consistently allowed.

This is why passivity is not harmless. What is not defined will be influenced. What is not governed will be shaped by whatever is active within it. The question is not whether the realm will produce something. The question is who is establishing what it produces.

You are not here only to be affected by the environment. You are here to participate in what is established within it. Under God's authority, you are meant to influence what functions, what holds, and what continues.

The realm may affect you, but you are not without authority in it. When aligned properly, you do not simply exist within the environment; you participate in determining what it becomes.

So, when the realm isn't responding to us as we want it to, expect it to, need it to, it is very likely that we have not been in our authority doing what we were supposed to do. It's kinda like, *"Preheat oven to 350 degrees Fahrenheit."* If you don't preheat the oven, it will not preheat itself. So the thing that should come next, baking those brownies or cookies from Chapter 1 won't happen because the preheating was not done.

When the environment is not responding the way it should—when it is not producing what you expect, what you need, or what aligns with what has been established—one of the first things to evaluate is not just the outcome, but the responsibility. Too often, the issue is not that nothing can happen. It is that what should have been established has not been established.

Authority is not automatic in its expression. It must be exercised. What is not actively defined will not define itself correctly.

This is where many misunderstand what they are experiencing. They assume the environment is simply "not responding," when in reality, it has never been properly set.

It is like an oven. If the instruction is to preheat to 350, the oven does not reach that temperature on its own. It must be set. It must be engaged. It must be brought into alignment with what is required before it can produce the desired or expected results.

If no one sets the temperature, the oven will remain at whatever state it is currently in. It will not correct itself. It will not anticipate the need. It will not prepare for what is coming.

In the same way, an environment does not automatically align with what should be produced. If it is not established, it will remain in its current condition or be shaped by whatever influence is active within it.

This is why lack of response is not always resistance. Sometimes it is simply the absence of establishment. What has not been set cannot produce.

What has not been brought into alignment cannot sustain what is expected from it. So, if you are changing locations or environments, consider very well where you are going before you go there, especially if you are moving there or planning to stay for a while. If you are a dry Christian what is there will remain and you will get pretty much what people get there. If you want to be an exception, then your behavior has to be different.

FOREIGN REALMS

Sometimes folks are in a foreign realm -- a realm they shouldn't be in and things don't work. OR they are in the right realm, but that realm hasn't been 'conditioned' to have the attributes and characteristics needed to make life and godliness work for that particular person. Sometimes people are in an environment that does not support them. They are operating in conditions that resist what they are trying to produce. In that case, things do not work—not because the effort is wrong, but because the environment is misaligned.

Other times, a person may be in the right environment, but that environment has not been conditioned. The necessary attributes, patterns, and reinforcement required to sustain what should happen are not yet established. So even though the location is correct, the conditions are not.

This is an important difference.

In one situation, the issue is placement. In the other, the issue is preparation.

A person can be positioned where they should be and still struggle, not because they are out of place, but because what surrounds them has not been brought into alignment with what is required.

This is why not every lack of results points to the same problem. Sometimes the solution is relocation. Sometimes the solution is conditioning.

If you are in an environment that consistently resists what should function, it may not be where you are meant to remain. But if you are in the right place and nothing is responding, then something needs to be established, reinforced, and maintained.

An environment does not automatically carry the characteristics you need. It reflects what has been built into it. So, the question is not just, "Where am I?" The question is also, "What has been established here?"

A person can be in the wrong place and struggle. Or they can be in the right place—and still need to build what allows it to work.

You cannot go to the desert and expect tropical plants to grow. The conditions do not support it. The soil, the moisture, and the climate are not aligned with what you are trying to produce.

In the same way, saltwater fish do not thrive in freshwater lakes and ponds. The issue is not the fish. The issue is the environment. What they require to live and function is not present.

It is a mistake to assume that if something is not working, something must be wrong with you; it may not be you at all. Sometimes, nothing is wrong with the effort, the intention, or even the design. The problem is the environment does not support the outcome.

Alignment matters. What you are trying to produce must match the conditions you are operating in. If the environment does not support it, it will not thrive, no matter how much effort is applied.

You cannot force growth where the conditions do not sustain it. You cannot expect the right results in the wrong environment. The question is not only what you are doing, the question is whether what surrounds you can support what you are trying to produce.

You can fly to the moon, but without oxygen, what do you plan to do there? The issue is not your ability to get there. The issue is whether the environment can support your life once you arrive.

This is why discernment is necessary. You must be able to recognize the environment you are in and respond to it accordingly. Not every space requires the same action. Not every condition responds the same way. You do not treat every environment the same. You discern it, and then you engage it.

Part of that engagement is what you allow and what you remove. When you minister—whether to God or to one another—you are not just participating in a moment. You are reinforcing conditions. You are helping to establish what is normal, what is sustained, and what continues.

This is how an environment becomes conditioned.

Just like the body maintains balance by keeping what is beneficial and removing what is harmful, the same principle applies. What is reinforced remains. What is allowed grows. What is resisted is weakened.

You do not leave an environment to regulate itself. You participate in what it becomes.

This is why discernment matters. You must recognize what is present, what is needed, and what must be reinforced or removed. An environment will respond to what is consistently maintained within it.

You are not just existing in an environment, you are participating in what it produces. So, the realm of the universe. the earth. wherever we live. our workplace. our house. our family. our anything needs to be ministered to so it can be kept in functioning condition to provide, produce, and deliver.

How long will it take to condition or recondition the realm?

Don't know. It's like breaking in a new pair of shoes – well sorta, but more complicated.

Every environment requires stewardship.

The universe, the Earth, the place you live, your workplace, your home, your family—none of these are meant to function unattended. They are not self-correcting systems that automatically maintain the conditions needed to provide, produce, and deliver.

They must be ministered to. This does not mean something mystical or complicated. It means they must be attended to, reinforced, and kept in proper condition so that what should function there can continue to function.

An environment does not remain stable on its own. It reflects what is consistently allowed, reinforced, and maintained within it. If it is neglected, it does not stay neutral. It begins to shift.

If it is not maintained, it does not hold its condition. It begins to deteriorate.

If it is not defined, it will be shaped by whatever influence is active within it. This is why stewardship matters.

You are not just living in these environments. You are responsible for what they become. What you reinforce strengthens them. What you ignore weakens them. What you allow establishes what will continue.

This applies everywhere. In your home, what you permit becomes normal. In your workplace, what is reinforced becomes the standard. In your family, what is maintained becomes the culture.

Nothing functions well without being tended to. When something stops producing, providing, or delivering, the question is not always what is missing. Sometimes the question is what has not been maintained.

You are not separate from your environment. You are participating in its condition. When you understand that, you stop waiting for things to work. You begin to maintain what makes them work.

Your lawn has weeds and bald spots; your neighbor's is lush and green, who put in the work? Your lawn has weeds and bald spots while your neighbor’s is lush and green. The question is not who has better grass. The question is who maintained their environment, because grass does not grow well by accident. Weeds do not ask permission. Bald spots do not announce themselves. They appear where something has not been maintained. A healthy lawn requires attention consistency reinforcement.

The lawn must be watered treated protected, and kept. The difference is not always the seed. It is the stewardship.

The same ground can produce completely different results depending on what is done with it. This is how environments work. What is maintained thrives. What is neglected deteriorates. Weeds grow where nothing is done to stop them. Growth happens where something is consistently done to support it.

When you see the difference, do not assume: one is lucky and the other is not. The difference is often simply that someone put in the work. What you refuse to maintain, you will eventually have to explain.

REALM WORK

Woe to those that are at ease in Zion.

What does one do in a realm? What is one's responsibility to 'his realm and does a person have authority to speak into other realms (as in other Earth realms)... like: when I get to work today, all things will work decent and in order... that sort of thing...?

A realm does not maintain itself. Every environment requires attention, reinforcement, and definition in order to function the way it should. Realm work is the ongoing responsibility of recognizing what is operating, establishing what should remain, and refusing what should not. It is not passive. It is not occasional. It is consistent.

To live in an environment is one thing. To steward it is another. Many exist within environments they have never taken responsibility for. They experience what is produced without ever addressing what is producing it. A realm responds to what is allowed, reinforced, and maintained. This means that what continues is not always what is intended. It is what has been permitted.

Realm work begins with recognition. You must be able to discern what is functioning, not just what is visible. What repeats, what resists, what responds, and what collapses are all indicators of what has been established. Without recognition, there is no clarity. Without clarity, there is no correction.

Once something is recognized, it must be addressed. This is where many hesitate. They observe patterns, but they do not interrupt them. They identify issues, but they do not define boundaries. Realm work requires interruption. What should not continue must be challenged. What should not remain must be restricted. What is left unaddressed will repeat, and what repeats will become established.

At the same time, what should function must be reinforced. It is not enough to remove what is wrong. Something must replace it. Order must be established. Consistency must be applied. What you want to see continue must be supported until it becomes the normal condition of the environment.

This is the responsibility of the one who occupies the space. Whether it is your home, your work, your family, or any environment you are assigned to, you are not there simply to experience what happens. You are there to participate in what is established. What you allow, what you reinforce, and what you maintain will determine what that environment produces.

This raises the question of authority. A person does not have unlimited authority everywhere, but they are not without influence. There is a difference between governing a space and entering one. In places where you have been given responsibility, your authority is direct. You define what is allowed. You establish what continues. You maintain what has been set.

In spaces where you do not have direct authority, your role is different. You do not control the environment, but you are not without responsibility. You carry alignment, consistency, and clarity into the space. You do not adopt what is misaligned. You do not reinforce what should not remain. You function correctly within it, and that alone creates distinction.

This is why a person can walk into a place and say, "Things will function in order today," and see a difference. Not because they control every person or every outcome, but because they are establishing alignment within their sphere of operation. They are setting conditions for what they will allow, what they will participate in, and what they will reinforce.

However, this is not about speaking randomly or attempting to control environments that have not been entrusted to you. It is about functioning within the authority you carry. What is established in you will affect what surrounds you, but it does not replace structure where you have no assignment.

Realm work is not about controlling everything. It is about governing what has been placed within your responsibility and maintaining alignment wherever you are.

Over time, what is consistently maintained will define the environment. What is reinforced will become normal. What is refused will lose its place. This is how environments change, not through a single moment, but through sustained responsibility.

You are not without influence. You are not without responsibility. The question is not whether something is happening in the environment. The question is what you are doing about it.

Realm work is not reacting to what is happening. It is establishing what is allowed to continue.

God put Adam & Eve in the Garden-- to 'dress the garden' -- mind the realm (I'll say)... everything worked for them in that realm. Then they sinned, got put out into a realm of weeds, thorns, thistles where things did not work. Did man get some authority over the Earth by say Deuteronomy by the Law-- by obedience, or did we have to wait until New Testament?

THE GARDEN is the place of original authority (Genesis 1:26–28, and Genesis 2:15). Man was given dominion, responsibility, and assignment. Dress it and keep it" = steward, guard, maintain. Everything in that environment responded to them because they were aligned, authorized, and in right relationship.

THE FALL and the BROKEN RESPONSE

- Genesis 3:17–19 Now the ground resists produces thorns requires toil

The Earth didn't disappear The **response changed Authority was not erased. It was disrupted and resisted."**

THE LAW - CONDITIONAL FUNCTION (Deuteronomy 28:1–14) Under the Law obedience → blessing disobedience → resistance rain responds, crops respond enemies respond land responds. Under the Law, the environment responded conditionally. Man did not regain full authority until after Jesus, but in the Old Testament access was tied to obedience It was not restored dominion; it was regulated function

Meaning you could see things work but only within strict alignment

4. THE NEW TESTAMENT — RESTORED POSITION

(Luke 10:19; Ephesians 2:6) Now authority is restored through Christ. Not earned by performance. maintained by law-keeping. Re-established by position and alignment in Him The Law managed response. Christ restored position.

Garden: everything responds Fall: resistance enters Law:
response becomes conditional. Christ authority is restored response is re-engaged through alignment did man regain authority in Deuteronomy? No—not fully. What happened instead? The environment responded… conditionally… based on obedience.

When was authority restored? In Christ. In the Garden, everything worked. After the Fall, everything resisted. Under the Law, things responded conditionally. In Christ, authority is restored.

Josephus the historian writes that Joseph was more prudent than his brothers... Joseph and who else were good or great stewards? God seems to love good stewards. That stands to reason since that was Adam and Eve's original assignment.

God entrusts more to those who steward well. Let's ground it biblically and keep it tight for your teaching voice.

JOSEPH — THE MODEL OF PRUDENCE AND STEWARDSHIP (Genesis 39:2–4; Genesis 41:39–41). Joseph didn't just interpret dreams—he **managed environments**. In Potiphar's house he prospered. In prison he was ordered and stable. In Egypt he was preserved through famine. Wherever he was placed, things worked. A steward does not wait for a good environment. They create function within the one they are given.

God trusted others as stewards.

ADAM (Original Assignment Genesis 2:15). Assigned to dress (cultivate) keep (guard). Stewardship was the *first job description.*

NOAH (Genesis 6:22) He followed instruction precisely, preserved life, entrusted with **continuity of the Earth**

ABRAHAM (Genesis 18:19). God trusted him to command his household, maintain order and righteousness, stewardship extended to **family and legacy.**

ELIEZER (Abraham's servant Genesis 24:2) Managed Abraham's entire estate. H was not the owner—but fully trusted

DAVID (1 Samuel 16:11–13) Before the throne he kept sheep faithfulness in **small stewardship → greater authority.**

NEHEMIAH (Nehemiah 2:17–18). He: rebuilt structure. restored order stewarded a **broken environment back to function**

NEW TESTAMENT (THE PRINCIPLE STATED CLEARLY). (Luke 16:10) Faithful in little → faithful in much. **God does not look for talent first. He looks for stewardship.** stewardship was the original assignment

So, it makes sense that God favors it rewards it builds on it **What God gives, He expects to be governed.**

GOD "LOVES" GOOD STEWARDS Because a good steward is obeying the first instruction that God gave man. A good steward does not waste what is given. A good steward does not neglect what is assigned. A good steward does not abandon what must be maintained. They **make things work.**

From Genesis to the New Testament the pattern never changes. There is an assignment. There must be stewardship and then there is increase.

What is your realm supposed to look like? Be like? Function like?

Thy kingdom come. Thy will be done in earth, as *it is* in heaven. (Matthew 6:10)

Actually, when Jesus taught the Disciples how to pray by teaching them the Lord's prayer, every word of that prayer is realm-building language.

HOW DO YOU RESPECT ANOTHER MAN'S REALM?

A man temporarily housed his brother during the COVID shut down. He had one requirement of his brother. He asked him, "On Tuesdays and Fridays will you take the trashcan to the curb and bring it back after the trash removal service has come?" One ask. He charged his brother not a penny for room, board, food, nothing. The brother refused to comply and the month-long fight ensued. One ask for a little stewardship. Now, the brother was in that man's house, in that man's realm… you should respect another man's realm.

Respecting another person's realm means recognizing where your authority ends where their responsibility begins. Respect is knowing where you have authority—and where you don't.

1. DON'T OVERRIDE THEIR STEWARDSHIP

If someone has been given responsibility over a space— their home, their work, their family, their assignment— you don't come in and **redefine it for them.**

Even if you see disorder, misalignment, things you would do differently, you don't take control. You don't correct what you have not been assigned to govern.

Don't build where you haven't been given permission. You don't: establish rules set expectations or try to shape outcomes in a space that is not yours to steward. Influence without permission becomes interference.

Carry your alignment—don't impose it. When you enter someone else's environment: you bring your order, your consistency, and your clarity, but you don't force it. You let what you carry speak through how you function. You don't push alignment. You demonstrate it.

Know the difference between presence and authority. You can be present in a room, included in a space, and invited into a setting, but that does not mean that you have authority over it Being in a space does not make you responsible for it.

Protect your own boundaries without controlling theirs. Respect goes both ways. You don't override their realm. You can set limits or step back without trying to control them. Respect does not necessarily mean agreement; it means you stay in your assignment.

as much as lieth in you, live peaceably… (romans 12:18)

… mind your own business (1 Thessalonians 4:11)

Respecting another man's realm is not silence, passivity, or agreement. It is right positioning. Honor another man's assignment, and stay faithful to your own.

he that is faithful with another man's will get or be given his own'

And if ye have not been faithful in that which is another

man's, who shall give you that which is your own? (Luke 16:12)

Before a person is entrusted with their own: they are tested in what belongs to someone else.

That starts early with a child and their toys. It may be seen in a student and a classroom. It is evident in an employee and a workplace. Stewardship is proven before it someone is promoted. From childhood up a child who takes care of what is given, respects what belongs to others, and maintains what they are allowed to use is already demonstrating, readiness for greater responsibility. This is not based on age, but because of faithfulness

What you do with what is not yours determines what will be entrusted to you.

When you are in another man's realm you don't control it. You don't own it. But you are being observed in how you function within it. Do you respect boundaries? Do you maintain order? Do you reinforce what is right? Do you avoid corrupting what is not yours? You are not just passing through another man's realm; you are being proven in it.

Many people want their own space, their own authority, their own "realm, but they have not been faithful in someone else's.

You don't step into your own simply by desire. You step into it by proven faithfulness. There must be preparation and opportunities with what belongs to others can promote you, demote you, or leave you stagnant.

God is not delaying or withholding, He is watching how you handle what is already in your hands. If you cannot maintain what is another man's, you are not ready to establish your own.

Stewardship is not a side principle in Scripture. It is the expectation of anyone given anything.

Adam and Eve weren't just placed in the Garden of Eden; they were trusted with a functioning environment.

People do come to Earth with different temperaments. When seeing an organized mind, even in a child, we must know that is probably innate in them; they were born with it. It isn't just good behavior, although it may be sign of having good parents. Either way, it's an early expression of order, care, and responsibility—the very things stewardship is made of.

A toddler who plays intentionally enjoys what they've been given, and then *puts it back in place* has the instinct to maintain what they've been entrusted with. It echoes the original design. Take it, use it, enjoy it, and then keep it in order. That's the Garden pattern in miniature.

Stewardship is not learned first. It is recognized—and then either developed or neglected. That child isn't thinking, "I must be a good steward," they're simply responding correctly to what they've been given. That's the purity of it. use it well, then keep it well.

Another child plays, scatters things everywhere, walks away and then can't figure out why they can't find their things when they want to play again. Same toys. Different response.

What is given does not determine the outcome. How it is handled does. Stewardship is not abstract it's not complicated. It shows up in toys, rooms, homes, lives, and realms. The one who puts things back in order… will always be trusted with more.

JESUS AND ORDER

Jesus did not enter environments and struggle with them; He entered—and things aligned. Not because He adjusted to what was there, but because what was there responded to Him.

Storms calmed, sickness left, demons recognized Him, disorder corrected itself. Jesus did not come under the environment. The environment came under Him. Because He was fully aligned, fully authorized, fully established, there was no conflict within Him. So, when He entered a space, what was out of order had to respond (Mark 4:39). Wind and sea obey (Luke 4:36). Demons obey, (Matthew 8:16), and sickness leaves.

Order was not something Jesus tried to create; it was something He carried. Jesus was not working on the environment; He was the standard, entering the environment. He did not negotiate with disorder; He corrected it.

We don't replicate Him in fullness…but we are called to align with Him. The more alignment there is, the more things begin to respond. You may not be the source of order— but you are called to carry alignment with it. Jesus could walk into any situation and establish order by being there because nothing in Him contradicted what He carried. What He carried was so established that disorder had no place to stand.

Creation didn't debate or hesitate. It recognized. So it should be for us, because in Christ, we function in Godly realms, especially our own. Creation does not resist what is fully aligned. It responds to it.

We don't fight the elements; we speak to them. As long as we are aligned, that is how it works. When alignment is complete, resistance loses its place. God is irresistible, Jesus is irresistible, all of Creation bows. Even the demons, the *spirit* world is subject to Him. Man is the only one with free will and the audacity to disobey the Only Living God, his Creator and Keeper.

By every word out of your mouth you are feeding or depleting your realm.

Creation bowing is the ultimate rẹsponse. Jesus did not force order; He did have to. Jesus walked in; Creation responded. Mountains crumbled. Trees withered, demons fled. Eyes and ears opened. Lame men walked and lepers were healed. Storms abated. Where alignment is established, Creation does not argue; it bows.

It is all of Creation that is waiting for the sons of God to appear. Here's the question: If, as a son of God Creation obeys you by obeying the voice of the Word of God, shouldn't everything else be an abiding request? Shouldn't everything else obey, happen, perform and function accordingly? As a son of God shouldn't your will also be aligned fully with the Will of the One who sent you?

Creation bows as the sons of God are manifest. Haven't you heard?

This is what happens there.

Where?

There.

All of Creation is waiting. Could this be why your realm is acting up? Have you become--, truly become a son of God?

If we are going to talk about Jesus and how things worked for Him then we will talk about how realms *move*. A realm is not fixed to a place. It is carried. It is maintained. It shows up wherever its conditions are present. A realm is not where you are, it is what you sustain.

Joseph was always Joseph no matter what his 10 older brothers wished for him. Wat worked for Joseph worked no matter where he was. It worked in Potiphar's house. It worked in the prison, and it worked back upstairs when he was promoted. It worked for all of Egypt during that hard seven-year famine. The location changed; the function did not.

Joseph didn't find good environments—he brought function into them.

That is the same WITH JESUS. conditions didn't control Him; He operated consistently. Where He was did not determine what happened—what He carried did.

This is portability. It says: Everywhere you go, there you are, but in a really good way.

If something only works in one place, only works under certain people, only works under perfect conditions, then it's not established. But if it works here, there, and under pressure, and under lack, then it is portable.

What is truly established will function wherever it is carried. You're not trying to find the perfect environment. Doesn't everyone sound good while singing in the shower? If you have to wait for the right conditions, you may not really be a good singer. But if you carry the condition with you, that's the true story. That is an established talent, gift, or anointing.

You stop looking for a realm when you realize you can carry one.

A realm doesn't have to be entered, accessed, or visited.

It can be maintained and brought into operation. If it only works somewhere, it's situational. If it works wherever you are, it's established.

ALL OF CREATION IS WAITING

The earnest expectation of the creature waiteth for the manifestation of the sons of God. (Romans 8:19)

Creation is waiting. *For*?

Manifestation.

Creation is not confused. It is waiting for clarity to appear in people. When an environment is unsettled… when things are inconsistent… when nothing seems to hold if it even works at all.

What is wrong with this environment? Is a good question. But the deeper question is, What is not yet established in me? An unsettled environment often reflects an unestablished carrier.

I am not saying that there is a connection between who you are and what responds.

Manifestation is what has been established. It is what has been presented and established in the physical realm. Why so? Because it started in the spiritual realm and then had to manifest into this one.

Have you become, truly become a son of God? Creation responds to what is established, not what is claimed. It is not enough to be called a son. Something must be established that creation can respond to.

Creation is waiting… for true alignment for order, for established authority. Creation is waiting for manifested sons of God to stand up in their authority and in their dominion and BE sons of God. Creation is waiting for what has been established to appear.

Where that establishment is present; response follows.

A realm isn't a cage—not a Faraday cage, not a wrestling enclosure like WWE Steel Cage Match. It's not something that physically traps you or locks you in.

A realm *is* an environment of consistent function. patterns repeat. responses are predictable, dependable. A realm doesn't trap you. It trains you to respond a certain way.

People *think* it's a cage because the same things keep happening. The same outcomes repeat. The same resistance shows up. So, it *feels* something like being stuck in a place, but what's actually happening is: pattern + reinforcement + no interruption.

Repetition can feel like captivity—until it's interrupted.

And there were four leprous men at the entering in of the gate: and they said one to another, Why sit we here until we die? (2 Kings 7:3)

A cage prevents exit. A realm influences response. In the Old Testament, there were lepers in the *realm* of the 'gate', starving or about to starve. They weren't physically locked up or sealed off. They weren't lame or unable to move. They were participating, following the 'rules' and maintaining their own punishment. Sometimes captivity is the signal that you need to do something else, something different, and maybe even the exact opposite of what you've been doing that either got you into captivity or that has kept you in captivity. Those lepers could move about, but there were rules and laws that kept them at the gate.

So, they simply remained there.

You don't escape a realm—you change what is allowed within it.

Even when someone feels stuck, movement is still possible. Adam and Eve were spiritually dead after they sinned, but they were still moving around as if they weren't dead. Until Jesus, though there was no way to fully come back from being locked out of realms of productivity, provision, and relationship except by the Law. A person had to strictly obey the Law in hopes of getting release from whatever his crime, punishment or captivity was.

No realm that the devil has authority in, speaks into or has control over will be kind to man; he hates man. So, Adam and Eve are now pushed out into that realm and that's when all the troubles start, or hadn't you noticed? Before Jesus there was no way to change that realm, even by microns and inches. You are not locked in. You are still responding—and that can be changed.

So, to 'rescue' someone from a 'realm' is really to give them permission to stop feeling or doing the things they do or feeling the way they feel that makes them continue patterns. (I won't say this, but like a hypnosis that says, 'sleep, sleep,' so the person shuts down part of their being and begin to function on minimal instead of their full being.) It is to set them back into their right alignment, their authority so they can speak to their own lives, live, move, have being and benefit from the power of their words, change their environment and atmosphere. It is so they can create a Godly realm overlaying and canceling out a demonic, hostile realm that was established for them because of their sin and sin nature.

You don't rescue someone from a realm as if you are pulling them out of a place. You help them recognize what they've been participating in and give them a way to respond differently. Jesus did that for us.

And when I passed by thee, and saw thee polluted in thine own blood, I said unto thee when thou wast in thy blood, Live; yea, I said unto thee when thou wast in thy blood, Live. (Ezekiel 16:6)

Change doesn't come from being removed, it comes from responding differently. People stay in patterns because something feels familiar, justified, or feels automatic. They stay when they feel powerless in the situation. They continue in the same response… well, that's just the way it is.

Is it? Jesus might say.

New thing, new creation, New Covenant, Better Blood. *Be ye conformed* (Romans 12:2). Patterns continue where responses don't change.

People can get used to functioning at a reduced level, not questioning, not interrupting, not challenging what's happening. This is oppression and the people have basically given up and given in, in either order.

What is repeated without interruption becomes normal—even when it limits you.

So, what does help looks like showing them their condition. Showing them what's happening

- what's repeating
- what they're agreeing with

And then giving them permission + clarity to change it. You don't just pull someone out of a pattern—you help them see they don't have to continue it. Else they will fall back into it.

awakening + interruption + new response

Freedom begins when a person realizes they can respond differently. Whom the Son sets free is free indeed.

In that long-standing or sudden or heavy oppression the oppressor may start something (destructive) and a human may do the rest of the damage themselves... Sometimes harm starts outside a person… but it continues through what gets repeated inside. What begins as pressure can become pattern if it isn't interrupted.

Something negative happens it creates a reaction the reaction gets repeated, maybe even escalated. the repetition becomes normal. This is survival mode. Over time the pattern sustains itself as the person makes futile attempts to either escape or just to stay alive in the oppression.

The initial harm may not be your fault, but the continuation can become your responsibility.

You are not responsible for what started it. But you are responsible for what continues. Think about it, this is actually good news Because if everything is external only then a person has no control, whatsoever. But if something continues through patterns, responses, reinforcement, then it can be changed.

What you can interrupt, you can change. fear → avoidance → more fear rejection → withdrawal → isolation stress → overreaction → more conflict

Not because the person *wants* it… but because it's become the pattern. uninterrupted patterns continue the damage. What isn't interrupted doesn't stop.

SPEAK, DON'T SPEAK

You don't unlock people—you help them see they can turn the key. basically people create their own realms (or they are supposed to) but if they let wrong people speak over or into their lives (intensely enough, long enough, or with a certain authority or people they give deference to) those people can affect a man's realm. Remember the stronger or more authoritative realm can overtake a weaker one.

People don't "create realms" out of nowhere, they build environments in their lives through what they accept, repeat, reinforce. Your environment is shaped by what you consistently allow.

Other people don't control your life by default, but they can influence it when you listen repeatedly, accept their words as Truth, or give them and their words weight or authority. Over time: their input becomes part of your internal pattern.

What you repeatedly agree with begins to shape how you live. What is being described here is not control. It is influence that becomes internalized. When someone speaks doubt or even an accusation, you repeat it. Even in attempting to defend yourself if you repeat the mistake or lie they have spoken over you--, you have just repeated it.

Words that come out of your own mouth, even negative words can be very damaging against you and will allow wrong things into your realm. When someone sets a low standard and you adopt it that can negatively affect your realm and your life. When someone normalizes dysfunction and you allow or tolerate it, that will not build Godly structure.

Eventually if all these wrong things are internalized and it will begin to feel like *your own thinking.* What starts as someone else's voice can become your default response.

People cannot just take over your life unless you give them the key to your life. Do not open up your heart and soul to just anyone. If you walk into soul ties, nets, traps and entanglements and do nothing about it, this is you deciding what you will allow.

You can question what you've accepted. interrupt what's not helping. replace it with something better. Replace it with the Word of Truth, the Word of God. Do not let evil imaginations color your realm or your life. You don't have to keep what you once accepted. Rise up in your own authority, govern your own life and shape your environment yourself. Guard what you accept—because what you accept will eventually shape how you live.

WARFARE DECLARATION

This is not a moment of reflection. This is a moment of decision.

In the Name of Jesus Christ, I refuse to continue in environments that contradict what God is establishing in me.

I will no longer normalize resistance, tolerate confusion, or adapt to what is not aligned.

What has been sustained without question, I now bring into order.

Every pattern that has been allowed to repeat without interruption, I confront it now.

Every environment that has delayed, diminished, or resisted what God has placed in me, I withdraw my agreement.

I break alignment with confusion, lack, disorder, and sustained resistance.

I will not participate in what weakens what I am called to establish.

Let every environment I have tolerated without discernment be exposed by Truth.

Let every pattern that has operated without challenge be interrupted now.

I will not continue in what does not respond to what God has spoken.

Where I have remained too long, I move. Where I have allowed too much, I correct it. Where I have adapted instead of governing, I take responsibility.

I establish clarity. I establish order. I establish alignment.

And I will maintain what I establish.

What God has authorized will not be resisted indefinitely. What has been delayed will not remain delayed. What has been misaligned will not continue unchallenged.

I am not subject to every environment. I am responsible for what I allow.

And from this point forward, I will not just react to outcomes. I will govern what produces them.

I will not remain in the wrong realm.

Amen.

Dear Reader

May the Lord richly bless you for acquiring and reading this book. Thank you for your support of this ministry.

Amen

Dr. Marlene Miles

If you enjoyed this book, here are some new releases

Christ of God (*The*) 3-book series

Christ of God, (*The*) Box Set, includes all 3books

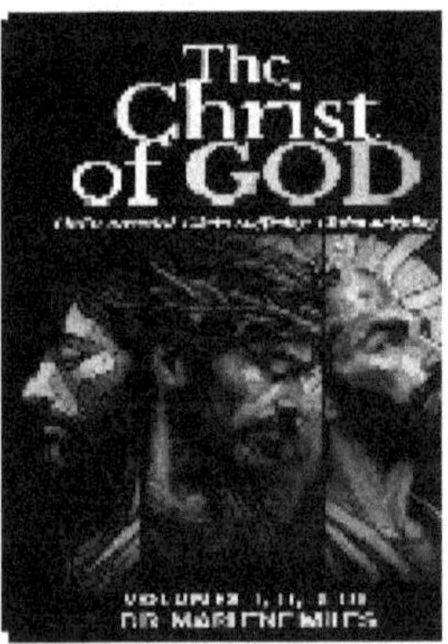

Other books on Authority:

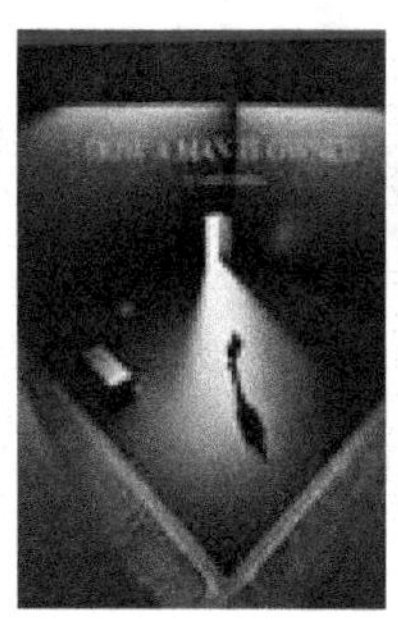

The Emptiers https://a.co/d/heio0dO

The Wasters https://a.co/d/5TG1iNQ

The Swallowers https://a.co/d/1jWhM6G

The Devourers: Why We Can't Have Nice Things https://a.co/d/87Tejbf

Spiritual Thieves https://a.co/d/eqPPz33

Prayerbooks by this author

There are some books that are only prayers. You just open up the book and pray.

Prayers Against Barrenness: *For Success in Business and Life*

Fruit of the Womb: *Prayers Against Barrenness*

Beauty Curses, *Warfare Prayers Against*
https://a.co/d/5Xlc20M

Courts of Marriage: Prayers for Marriage in the Courts of Heaven *(prayerbook)* https://a.co/d/cNAdgAq

Courtroom Warfare @ Midnight *(prayerbook)*
https://a.co/d/5fc7Qdp

Demonic Cobwebs *(prayerbook)* https://a.co/d/fp9Oa2H

Every Evil Bird https://a.co/d/hF1kh1O

Gates of Thanksgiving

Spirits of Death, Hell & the Grave, Pass Over Me and My House

Throne of Grace: Courtroom Prayer

Warfare Prayer Against Poverty
https://a.co/d/bZ61lYu

FAKE FRIENDS: *Prayers Against Betrayers*

HOLIDAY WARFARE Prayer Manual (humorous) Surviving Family Gatherings All Year Long (without catching a case)

SOUL TIE Prayer Manual (The) Part of a 3-part series including a workbook.

MAD at DADDY Prayer Manual – part of a 3-part series including a workbook.

Healing the Sibling & Relative Wound Prayer Manual

Healing the Father-Son Wound Prayer Manual

Breaking Curses of the Mother Prayer Manual

Other books by this author

Abundance of Jesus (The) https://a.co/d/5gHJVed

AK: The Adventures of the Agape Kid

Already Married in the Spirit: *Why You May Not Be Married in the Natural*

AMONG SOME THIEVES https://a.co/d/dkYT4ZV

Ancestral Powers

Anti-Marriage, *The Spirit of*

Backstabbers https://a.co/d/gi8iBxf

Barrenness, *Prayers Against* https://a.co/d/feUltIs

Battlefield of Marriage, *The*

BEHAVE: *Be, Then Have*

Beware of the Dog: Prayers Against Dogs in the Dream.

Bless Your Food: *Let the Dining Table be Undefiled*
https://a.co/d/6oPMRDv

Blindsided: *Has the Old Man Bewitched You?*
https://a.co/d/5O2fLLR

Break Free from Collective Captivity

Broken Spirits & Dry Bones

By Means of a Whorish Father

Caged Life: Get Out Alive! https://a.co/d/bwPbksX

Casting Down Imaginations

Christ of God (*The*) 3-book series

Christ of God, (*The*) Box Set, includes all three books

Churchzilla, The Wanna-Be, Supposed-to-be Bride of Christ https://a.co/d/eAf5j3x

Collateral Damage: *When What Happened Spiritually Was Your Fault*

Demonic Cobwebs (prayerbook)

Demonic Time Bombs

Demons Hate Questions

Devil Loves Trauma, *The*

Devil Weapons: Unforgiveness, Bitterness,…

The Devourers: Thieves of Darkness 2

Do Not Swear by the Moon

Don't Refuse Me, Lord (4 book series)

https://a.co/d/idP34LG

Dream Defilement

The Emptiers: *Thieves of Darkness, 1*
https://a.co/d/5I4n5mc

Entanglements: Illegal Knots Limiting Your Life

Evil Touch

Failed Assignment

Fantasy Spirit Spouse https://a.co/d/hW7oYbX

FAT Demons (The): *Breaking Demonic Curses*
https://a.co/d/4kP8wV1

The Fold (5-book series)

- The Fold (Book 1)
- Name Your Seed (Book 2)
- The Poor Attitudes of Money (3)
- Do Not Orphan Your Seed (4)
- For the Sake of the Gospel (5)
- My Sowing Journal

Gang Ups: Touch Not God's Anointed

Gathered: No Longer Scattered
https://a.co/d/1i5DPIX

Getting Rid of Evil Spiritual Food

https://a.co/d/i2L3WYQ

got HEALING? Verses for Life

got LOVE? Verses for Life https://a.co/d/8seXHPd

got HOPE? Verses for Life

got money? https://a.co/d/g2av41N

Has My Soul Been Sold? https://a.co/d/dyB8hhA

Here Come the Horns: *Skilled to Destroy* https://a.co/d/cZiNnkP

Hidden Sins: Hidden Iniquity

https://a.co/d/4Mth0wa

How to Dental Assist

How to Dental Assist2: Be Productive, Not Wasteful

How To Stay Prayed Up

How to STOP Being a Blind Witch or Warlock

I Take It Back

In Multiplying I Will Multiply Thee

Into Freedom:

Irresistible: Jesus' Triumphal Entry
https://a.co/d/d09IfEC

KNOW YOUR BATTLE: Stop Swinging Blindly — and Win Against Opponents, Adversaries & Enemies (Workbook) https://a.co/d/eOwFKlV

Legacy

Let Me Have A Dollar's Worth
https://a.co/d/h8F8XgE

Level the Playing Field

Living for the NOW of God https://a.co/d/6bK5duE

Lose My Location https://a.co/d/crD6mV9

Love Breaks Your Heart

Mad At Daddy: Healing Father-Wounds that Affect Motherhood (book, workbook & prayer manual)

Made Perfect In Love

Mammon https://a.co/d/29yhMG7

Man Safari, *The*

Marriage Ed.: *Rules of Engagement & Marriage*

Made Perfect in Love

Money Hunters: Beware of Those

Money on the Altar https://a.co/d/4FqJ2Nr

Mulberry Tree, *The* https://a.co/d/9nR9rRb

Motherboard (The)- *Soul Prosperity Series*

Name Your Seed

Occupy: *Until I Return* https://a.co/d/bZ7ztUy

One Defining Day: *A Day When Dreams Come True*

Opponent, Adversary, or Enemy?: Fight The Right Battle with the Right Weapons https://a.co/d/byQqEE2 & companion workbook: Know Your Battle

Plantation Souls

Players Gonna Play

PLEAD YOUR CASE book & Study Guide

Portals: Shut the Front Door: Prayers to Close Evil Portals.

Power Money: Nine Times the Tithe

https://a.co/d/gRt41gy

The Power to Get Wealth https://a.co/d/e4ub4Ov

Powers Above

The Robe, Part 1, The Lessons of Joseph

The Robe, Part II, The Lessons of Joseph

Scarcity Mindset (The)

Seasons of Grief

Seasons of Rest (forthcoming)

Seasons of Siege: God Is Coming

Seasons of Waiting

Seasons of War

Second Marriage, Third--, *Any Marriage*

https://a.co/d/6m6GN4N

Seducing Spirits: Idolatry & Whoredoms

https://a.co/d/4Jq4WEs

Shut the Front Door: *Prayers to Close Portals*
https://a.co/d/cH4TWJj

Siege: *God Is Coming*

Sift You Like Wheat

The Silences of God:

Six Men Short: What Has Happened to all the Men?

SLAVE

Sleep Afflictions & Really Bad Dreams https://a.co/d/f8sDmgv

Soul Prosperity soul prosperity series 3

https://a.co/d/5p8YvCN

Soul Ties: How Soul Ties Form, and How To Break Them (book, workbook & prayer manual)

Souls In Captivity

The Spirit of Anti-Marriage

The Spirit of Poverty https://a.co/d/abV2o2e

Spiritual Thieves https://a.co/d/eqPPz33

StarStruck- Triangular Power series.

SUNBLOCK- Triangular Power series.

The Swallowers: *Thieves of Darkness,* 3

Take It Back

This Is NOT That: How to Keep Demons from Coming at You

Thrones

Time Is of the Essence

Too Many Wives: *Why You Have Lady Problems*

Tormenting Spirits https://a.co/d/dAogEJf

Toxic Souls

Triangular Power *(series),* Powers Above, SUNBLOCK, Do Not Swear by the Moon, STARSTRUCK

TRIBE: *What Covenants Are Governing You…?*

Unbreak My Heart: *Don't Let Me Die*

Uncontested Doom

Ungovered Hunger: How Unchecked Appetite Dismantles Authority

Unguarded Hours, *The*

Unseen Life, *The* (forthcoming)

Upgrade: How to Get Out of Survival Mode Toxic Souls (Book 2 of series) , Legacy (Book 3 of series)

The Wasters: *Thieves of Darkness,* Bk 2 https://a.co/d/bUvI9Jo

What Have You to Declare? What Do You Have With You from Where You've Been?

When I Was A Child, *I Prayed As a Child*

When the Devourer is Rebuked https://a.co/d/1HVv8oq

When The Table Is Set Against You

WTH? Get Me Out of This Hell https://a.co/d/a7WBGJh

The Wilderness Romance ***(series)*** This series is about conducting a Godly relationship and marriage with someone who is a Wilderness person. ***The Social Wilderness***

- ***The Sexual Wilderness***
- ***The Spiritual Wilderness***

Other Series

The Fold (a series on Godly finances)

https://a.co/d/4hz3unj

Soul Prosperity Series https://a.co/d/bz2M42q

Spirit Spouse books

https://a.co/d/9VehDSo

https://a.co/d/97sKOwm

Battlefield of Marriage, The

https://a.co/d/eUDzizO

Players Gonna Play

https://a.co/d/2hzGw3N

Sent Spirit Spouse (can someone send you a spirit spouse? This book is not yet released.)

Matters of the Heart, Made Perfect in Love https://a.co/d/70MQW3O , Love Breaks Your Heart https://a.co/d/4KvuQLZ, Unbreak My Heart https://a.co/d/84ceZ6M Broken Spirits & Dry Bones https://a.co/d/e6iedNP

Thieves of Darkness series

The Emptiers https://a.co/d/heio0dO

The Wasters https://a.co/d/5TG1iNQ

The Swallowers https://a.co/d/1jWhM6G

The Devourers: Why We Can't Have Nice Things
https://a.co/d/87Tejbf

Spiritual Thieves

Red Flags: The Track Is Not Safe (book & workbook)

Triangular Powers https://a.co/d/aUCjAWC

Upgrade (series) *How to Get Out of Survival Mode* https://a.co/d/aTERhXO

We Get Along, Right? Compatibility for Couples – (book & workbook)

Dr. Marlene Miles is a teacher, author, and spiritual thinker known for her grounded, discerning approach to prayer and spiritual formation. Her work emphasizes clarity, restraint, and maturity in faith—helping believers move beyond emotionalism and performance into a steady, practiced walk with God.

With a deep respect for Scripture and a practical understanding of daily life, Dr. Miles writes for those who want their prayer life to be formed, not dramatized. Her teaching encourages spiritual maintenance, discernment, and responsibility—so faith remains strong not only in crisis, but in everyday living.

www.ingramcontent.com/pod-product-compliance
Lightning Source LLC
LaVergne TN
LVHW010703110826
845149LV00014B/3203

* 9 7 8 1 9 7 1 9 3 3 5 5 9 *